A Louisiana Christmas

Heritage Recipes and Hometown Celebrations

Carol Stubbs and Nancy Rust

PELICAN PUBLISHING COMPANY
GRETNA 2014

First edition, 2011
First Pelican edition, 2014

The word "Pelican" and the depiction of a pelican are
trademarks of Pelican Publishing Company, Inc., and are
registered in the U.S. Patent and Trademark Office.

ISBN: 9781455619795
E-book ISBN: 9781455619801

Page 1: Chocolate Fudge, Desserts, page 160

Printed in the United States of America
Published by Pelican Publishing Company, Inc.
1000 Burmaster Street, Gretna, Louisiana 70053

To all who hold the wonder of Christmas in their hearts

Crystal Star, Activities and Crafts, page 182

Special thanks to Jeffery Gueno. Over a long period of time he and the late Frank Hanley collected the exquisite Neapolitan figures and setting for the Hanley-Gueno Presepio. It is from this amazing and beautiful exhibit that we found our inspiration and theme for this book.

Hanley-Gueno Neopolitan Presepio
Cathedral of St. John the Evangelist Museum
Lafayette, Louisiana

TABLE OF CONTENTS

ACKNOWLEDGEMENTS

This book has been a leap of faith, a journey by two friends across a state rich in cultural influences and traditions. Both of us are writers, and we are daughters, sisters, wives, mothers, grandmothers and aunts who have experienced the joy of Christmas in Louisiana from many angles. Our goal was to create a book that captures the best of the holidays in a state that loves to celebrate and to help busy people find peace, joy and love in timeless holiday traditions and meals shared with family and friends.

We are appreciative of the wonderful response we have received from everyone we contacted about the book. Our job was made easier through the generosity and spirit of camaraderie we found throughout our unique state.

Special thanks to our good friend, Ann Palombo, who began this work with us and contributed several recipes and much of the information for the section, Esprit de Noel. She also made contacts to help us find some of the best holiday fare in Louisiana. We are so grateful to our friends and family, as well as to the many chefs, cooks, businesses and restaurants who graciously shared some of their favorite holiday recipes.

We are grateful to Andre Andrepont for his expert help in designing the cover. And we want to express our thanks to the talented photographers who capture the intriguing beauty of Louisiana. Thanks to Bryan Tuck, who took the beautiful photographs of the Hanley-Gueno Presepio at the Cathedral of St. John in

Lafayette. And to Mickey Delcambre, New Iberia photographer, for his beautiful landscape photographs seen in this secton and on the cover. Thanks also to the tourism and convention bureaus who shared information and photos from their region: Shreveport-Bossier Convention and Tourist Bureau, New Orleans CVB, Louisiana Office of Tourism and Natchitoches Area Convention and Visitors Bureau. Special thanks to Michelle Chapuis-Broussard, Drew Stubbs, Acadian Village and Oak Alley Plantation for sharing photos and to the late Bob Maeser, Carol's father, who provided the pen and ink illustrations.

We could not have done this without the love and support of our husbands and our sons and daughters. Special thanks to them for their patience, helpful ideas and willingness to eat holiday food all through the year as we tested recipes.

Merci Beaucoup!

Oak Tree on Crochet Road, Iberia Parish, Courtsey of Mickey Delcambre

INTRODUCTION

Christmas in Louisiana is unique. It embraces warm hospitality, incomparable food, a rich musical heritage and cultural diversity. It's the time to gather with family and friends and celebrate the age-old Advent traditions of joy, peace, love and hope. In a state known for its festivals and celebrations, Christmas brings a special joie de vivre. From the bayous in the south to the pine forests in the north, holiday events uniquely combine the allure of Louisiana with the spirit of Christmas.

The familiar sights, sounds and tastes of Christmas are wrapped in traditions brought here centuries ago by early settlers and still honored today. Events, beginning with the lighting of Advent candles, bring all ages out in reverence and celebration. There are traditional candlelight services, evenings of caroling and live Nativity performances, as well as festivities that capture the aura of Louisiana. Among the cultural favorites are boat parades on the bayou, Christmas Eve bonfires along the levee and lavish Réveillon meals after midnight Mass.

Whether with the flickering lights at the St. Lucy Festival in St. Martinville, the fine Eighteenth-Century Presepio at the Cathedral of St. John in Lafayette, the explosion of light and sound from fireworks over the

Cane River in Natchitoches or the smell of evergreens in a historic plantation on the River Road, Louisiana celebrates Christmas in distinctly meaningful and remarkable ways.

A Louisiana Christmas lists some of the major Christmas events in the state and includes recipes and sample menus, as well as ideas for gifts and family activities. Chefs, businesses, restaurants and home cooks contributed a wide variety of recipes. They range from quick and easy preparations for busy days to elaborate dishes for special occasions.

It's been said Louisiana is more a gumbo than a melting pot, with each culture adding its own rich flavor or spicy influence to the mix, and at no time is that more evident than during the Christmas season. We hope this book inspires everyone to celebrate Christmas in Louisiana style, taking time to enjoy the season with family, friends, faith, food and fun.

Joyeux Noël!

Carrot Cake, Desserts, page 142

LES FÊTES DE NOËL

Louisiana attracts visitors from around the world who want to experience its unique heritage and cultures. Every parish (county) has treasured Christmas traditions and events. Les Fêtes de Noël is a regional guide to a sampling of the exciting and diverse celebrations in the state. Contact information is included so you can get up-to-date details about times and locations.

Festivals
Festival season is at its height in the fall, building up to November with *Louisiana Main to Main, a Cultural Roadshow,* followed by holiday events in December. In Natchitoches, Turn on the Holidays is a *Main to Main* event that kicks off the annual Festival of Lights as more than 300,000 lights and riverfront displays are turned on. Take a road trip through Louisiana and fill your holidays with lights, food, fun and music.
www.crt.state.la.us/maintomain;
www.louisianatravel.com

Christmas Bird Count
Louisiana is one of the most important bird habitat locations in the nation, and coastal cities like Grand Isle, the site of the first Louisiana bird trail, are prime places to birdwatch. The terrain and climate of the state attract a variety of birds, and there are trails located along the Gulf Coast and throughout the state. The National Audubon Society's annual Christmas Bird Count, dating back to 1900, records the numbers of birds along the Gulf Coast and throughout the nation. Information from the annual count is used to help protect species and their habitats.
www.louisianatravel.com/louisiana-birding-trails

REGIONAL MAP OF LOUISIANA

www.louisianatravel.com

Photo courtesy of Oak Alley Plantation, www.oakalleyplantation.com

Lighting the bonfire at Oak Alley Plantation

PLANTATION COUNTRY
Baton Rouge, St. Francisville, River Road

Christmas in the Country

The charming town of St. Francisville looks festive with
millions of lights and historic plantations decorated for
the season. The winter landscape features moss-draped
oaks and a variety of colorful camellias. Activities include
shopping in wonderful boutiques brimming with art and
antiques, a tree lighting, home tours, caroling, musical
entertainment, a Christmas parade and a live nativity.
www.stfrancisvillefestivals.com

Plantations in St. Francisville

Oakley House: Audubon State Historic Site. West
Indies-style house where John J. Audubon painted 32 of
his famous bird pictures. Candlelight tours, as well as
daily tours.
11788 LA 965, 225-635-3739, www.stfrancisville.us

Butler Greenwood: Former indigo and cotton
plantation with lovely English gardens in Eighteenth-
Century style. Daily tours. B&B.
8345 US Hwy 61, 225-635-6312,
www.butlergreenwood.com

Catalpa: Late Victorian cottage-style house with an oak
alley in unusual elliptical shape. Open by appointment.
Catalpa Ln., 225-635-3372, www.stfrancisville.us

Cottage: Plantation home with spacious galleries,
outbuildings and ancient oak trees. Daily tours. B&B.
10528 Cottage Ln., 225-635-3674,
www.cottageplantation.com

Greenwood: Magnificent columned home that has been featured in several movies. Special events. Daily tours. B&B. 6838 Highland Rd., 800-259-4475, www.greenwoodplantation.com

Rosedown: State historic site with an oak alley, lovely and extensive gardens, outbuildings and main house. Daily tours.
12501 Hwy.10, 888-376-1867, www.stfrancisville.us

The Myrtles: Considered one of America's most beautiful haunted houses. Historical tours and mystery tours. B&B.
7747 US Hwy. 61, 225-635-6277, www.myrtlesplantation.com

Christmas in the Red Stick
Downtown Baton Rouge lights up a 35-foot Christmas tree and half a million lights to kick off a month of spectacular holiday events throughout the capital city. The downtown festival features imaginative decorations, visits with Santa in the historic state capital, street performers, caroling and bands, train rides and delicious food. December events include symphony concerts, the Holiday Art Walk, theater performances and a parade.
225-389-5520, www.visitbatonrouge.com

Historical Holidays
Magnolia Mound Plantation in Baton Rouge is decorated for the holidays. The house is open for tours, which include information on historical celebrations and songs. Special event is the French Creole Christmas with traditional activities, music and a bonfire.
2161 Nicholson Dr., 225-343-4955, www.brec.org

Great River Road

Step back in time as plantations along the 70-mile River Road are decorated in classic Christmas style.

Oak Alley: Greek Revival-style house with a quarter-mile canopy of ancient live oaks. Annual Christmas Bonfire Party with guides in antebellum dress, dinner, a parade to the levee for the bonfire, caroling, entertainment and dancing. Guided tours. B&B.
3645 Hwy. 18, Vacherie; 800-442-5539,
www.oakalleyplantation.com

Houmas House: Southern splendor at this Greek Revival home and gardens. Special events and tours.
40136 LA Hwy 942, Darrow; 225-473-9380,
www.houmashouse.com

Destrehan Plantation: A majestic plantation established in 1787. Historical demonstrations and tours.
13034 River Rd, Destrehan; 877-453-2095,
www.destrehanplantation.org

St. Joseph Plantation: Sugar plantation built in raised Creole style. Tours and special events.
3535 LA Hwy 18, Vacherie; 225-365-4078,
www.stjosephplantation.com

Laura Plantation: Creole sugar plantation where Brer Rabbit tales were recorded. Special tours and events.
2247 LA Hwy 18, Vacherie; 225-265-7690,
www.lauraplantation.com

Nottoway Plantation and Resort: Majestic three-story mansion with 22 massive columns. Tours and special events. B&B. 31025 Louisiana Hwy. 1, White Castle;
866-527-6884, 225-545-2730, www.nottoway.com

Judge Felix Poché Plantation: Victorian-style home and extensive grounds with RV, camping and B&B facilities. 6554 LA Hwy 44, Convent; 225-562-7728, www.pocheplantation.com

Evergreen Plantation: Most intact plantation complex in the South. Tours and special events. 4677 Hwy. 18, Edgard; 985-497-3837, www.evergreenplantation.org

San Francisco Plantation: Opulent, colorful, galleried Creole-style house. Tours and special events. 2646 LA Hwy 44, Garyville; 985-535-2341, www.sanfranciscoplantation.org

Christmas Eve Bonfires

One of the many Christmas traditions in Louisiana is lighting bonfires along the levees on Christmas Eve. Tradition states that the huge fires light the way for the Cajun Papa Noël rushing through the bayous on a pirogue or for people going to midnight Mass. In St. John and Ascension parishes and in the St. James Parish towns of Lutcher, Gramercy and Paulina, communities gather each year to build huge bonfires along the river levee. Precisely at 7 p.m. fire chiefs give a signal, and all of the bonfires are lit.

Festival of Bonfires

For those who want to experience the thrill of the bonfire before Christmas Eve, the town of Lutcher hosts the annual Festival of Bonfires the second weekend in December. Each night of the festival one bonfire is lit. During the day, there are family-oriented activities, live music and traditional Cajun foods. www.festivalofthebonfires.org; www.stjamesparish.com

Photo courtesy of Andrew Stubbs, www.amstubbs.com

St. Louis Cathedral in historic Jackson Square
New Orleans

GREATER NEW ORLEANS
New Orleans, Plaquemines, Grand Isle

Christmas New Orleans Style
New Orleans goes all out for Christmas. The city,
renowned for lavish parties and celebrations, takes on a
special glow in December with numerous activities and
things to see. In the French Quarter, join carolers
singing by candlelight in Jackson Square or look for Papa
Noël strolling through the historic streets. Enjoy tours of
beautifully decorated homes, and see the festive hotels.
Christmas is a magical time in the Crescent City.
www.neworleansonline.com

Celebration in the Oaks
Visit City Park in New Orleans for Celebration in the
Oaks, one of the city's most treasured events. It's held in
the Botanical Garden and the park with its century-old
moss-laden live oaks. At Christmas, the park is filled
with millions of lights and has displays and activities for
all ages. Special features include a poinsettia tree in the
Botanical Garden, a laser light show set to New Orleans-
style Christmas music, a multi-media exhibit of the
Cajun Night Before Christmas, plus rides and nightly
entertainment.
www.celebrationintheoaks.com

Hanukkah Celebrations
New Orleans celebrates Hanukkah on the Riverwalk
with traditional food, music and a lighting of the state's
largest Menorah. Chanukah on the Avenue is celebrated
uptown at Temple Sinai on St. Charles Ave. with
Menorah lighting, music and food.
504-782-2804, www.nola.com

Cathedral Concerts

St. Louis Cathedral in Jackson Square, the oldest continuously active Roman Catholic cathedral in the country, hosts a series of free concerts in December. Local choirs, jazz ensembles and legendary artists are featured in a concert series that brings joy to the season. Check the website for scheduling information. www.stlouiscathedral.org; www.neworleansonline.com

Réveillon

Historically, Réveillon is a long, lavish meal with family and friends, usually served after midnight Mass on Christmas Eve. The word Revéillon comes from the French word, *reveil*, to waken, and the meal was an elaborate way to break the fast after attending Mass. In early New Orleans, most of the community celebrated this tradition involving fine food and libation and parties that sometimes lasted through the night. The tradition continues today in a new form as restaurants throughout the city celebrate Revéillon with special menus including three or four-course prix fixe meals. www.neworleansonline.com

Holiday of Lights

Louisiana's first rails-to-trails conversion project is a nature trail paradise running from Slidell to Covington. Christmas lights, music and activities along the trail include a Holiday of Light celebration at the trailhead in Covington, Christmas under the Stars in Slidell and Winter on the Water in Mandeville. www.louisiananorthshore.com

Shopping

For window shopping or buying gifts, New Orleans is the place to be. Eclectic shops on Magazine Street; fine antiques, art galleries and boutiques in the French Quarter; familiar stores and upscale shops along the Riverwalk and in Canal Place are a few of the interesting places to shop. Museums and attractions have gift shops, and there are interesting local bookstores and specialty stores featuring everything from hats to masks. The French Market in the French Quarter and the Crescent City Market offer the best of home-grown Louisiana, and there are restaurants and cafés throughout the city where you can relax and take in the Christmas ambiance.

Downtown Christmas Lighting

Ponchatoula is known as the Strawberry Capital of the World with strawberries available from November to April. In December it's time for Christmas lights and special events, which include shopping in "America's Antique City."
www.ponchatoulachamber.org

Photo courtesy of Shreveport-Bossier Convention and Tourist Bureau

The Louisiana Boardwalk on the Holiday Trail of Lights

SPORTSMAN'S PARADISE
North Louisiana: Shreveport, Monroe, Ruston

Holiday Trail of Lights: Fa La La Louisiana!

Follow a glittering trail of lights through the cities of Shreveport-Bossier, Monroe-West Monroe, Alexandria-Pineville, Minden and Natchitoches. The lights illuminate two Louisiana regions, Sportsman's Paradise and Crossroads, connected through I-20 and I-49. Stop in the cities along the trail and enjoy great food, shopping and holiday entertainment. Special events include a spectacular Laser Light Show in Shreveport, dancing lights in Antique Alley in Monroe, an outstanding display of lights on Cane River at the Festival of Lights in Natchitoches, a Christmas parade, light displays and nutcrackers in Minden and holiday celebrations in Alexandria and Pineville. www.holidaytrailoflights.com

December on the Red Fireworks Festival

Enjoy spectacular firework displays Saturday nights in December on the riverfront in Shreveport. The riverfront includes casino action, shopping and dining in the Red River District. On the Bossier City side, the Louisiana Boardwalk is the state's largest lifestyle center with shopping, dining and entertainment. www.shreveportbossierfunguide.com

Christmas on the River

Monroe and West Monroe host a variety of community celebrations, including church pageants and plays, hay rides, carolers, Christmas Village at the Children's Museum, dancing lights, a PAWrade for pets and art contest trees, as well as plenty of shopping opportunities.
Monroe-West Monroe Convention & Visitors Bureau, 318-387-5691, 800-843-1872, www.christmasontheriver.org

Christmas at The Biedenharn

The Biedenharn Museum and El Song Gardens in Monroe are decked out for the holidays and have several special events in December. The site includes a historic home, formal English-style gardens, Bible Museum and Coca-Cola Museum.
800-362-0983, www.bmuseum.org

Christmas in Roseland

The Gardens of the American Rose Center in Shreveport is home to the national headquarters of the American Rose Society and includes 118 acres of rose gardens. In December the gardens are decorated with beautiful lights, displays and giant Christmas cards made by children. Nightly entertainment, a Roseland Express train and a wooden train exhibit offer fun for the family.
8877 Jefferson Paige Rd., 318-938-5534, www.ars.org

Christmas on Caddo Fireworks Festival

The family festival features a boat flotilla and visits with Santa, as well as light displays, entertainment and a spectacular fireworks show. Festival is held in Earl Williamson Park in Oil City.
www.christmasoncaddofireworks.com

Christmas in Minden

Celebrate all things German at the Fasching Fifth Season Celebration in November, a prelude to December when hundreds of nutcrackers are featured in displays, and thousands of Christmas lights illuminate city streets, parks and the historic district. Activities include a community chorus candlelight concert, art show, candlelight home tours, First Baptist Church Christmas concert and Christmas Eve service.
www.mindenusa.com

Wonderland in the Pines
Jonesboro creates a magical wonderland with millions of
Christmas lights each December. Events include carriage rides,
visits with Santa and a parade.
www.jacksonparishchamber.org

Christmas Tree Farms
Enjoy the fun of choosing a fresh tree at one of North
Louisiana's tree farms.

Pepper Tree Farm
2181 Hwy 557, Monroe
318-387-5172, www.peppertreefarm.net

Precious Memories Christmas Tree Farm
455 Glen Acres Rd., Calhoun
318-396-5113, www.preciousmemorieschristmastreefarm.com

Weaver's Christmas Tree Farm
2995 Jolly Napier Rd, Shreveport
318-636-6101, www.weaverschristmastreefarm.com

Photo courtesy of Natchitoches Convention & Visitors Bureau, www.natchitoches.net

Fireworks over Cane River at the Festival of Lights

CROSSROADS
Central Louisiana: Alexandria, Natchitoches, Toledo Bend

Christmas Festival and Festival of Lights
Natchitoches, the oldest permanent French settlement in Louisiana, goes all out to celebrate Christmas with the Festival of Lights and the Christmas Festival, one of the nation's oldest community-based holiday celebrations. What began in the late 1920s with a few strings of lights on Front Street has become a fantastic series of events. The Festival of Lights begins mid-November, with the Christmas Festival held the first weekend in December. There are special events all through the holidays, including spectacular light displays and fireworks over the Cane River, as well as boat parades, candlelight home tours, children's activities, arts and crafts, music and more.
800-259-1714, www.christmasfestival.com

Christmas Downriver and Holiday Tour of Homes
Head downriver for A Creole Christmas. Events include musical entertainment, educational programs and special tours at designated plantations in the Cane River National Creole Historical Park. Annual Holiday Tour of Homes is sponsored by the Natchitoches Historical Foundation.
800-259-1714, www.christmasfestival.com

Riverfront Christmas Display
Vidalia is a small town located across the Mississippi River from Natchez, Mississippi. The bridge between the two cities is beautifully lit at night, joining the two states. At Christmas, Vidalia takes advantage of its riverfront location with fireworks, lighting displays, trolley rides, Santa, music and more.
www.vidaliaconventioncenter.com

12 Days of Christmas

Alexandria celebrates Christmas with 12 Days of Christmas, an extravaganza of lights, entertainment and caroling. Christmas festivities in December include an old-fashioned Christmas at Kent Plantation House, a live nativity, musical performances, Holiday Safari with lights at the zoo and inspirational worship experiences.
318-442-9546, 800-551-9546, www.theheartoflouisiana.com

Christmas in the Park

West Park in Deridder turns into a winter wonderland with thousands of Christmas lights, snow village and Santa's Workshop. Enjoy a train ride and a cup of hot chocolate while waiting to see Santa.
337-396-4717, www.cityofderidder.org

Miracle on Washington Avenue

The dazzling Christmas celebration in Deridder includes a downtown Christmas festival with shopping, food and games for the kids.
337-463-5534, www.cityofderidder.org

Christmas on the Bayou Festival

Cottonport is located on Bayou Rouge where you can see one of the largest Christmas parades in the state. A Christmas festival and fireworks take place after the parade.
800-833-4195, www.travelavoyelles.com

Photo courtesy of Michelle Chapuis-Broussard
www.michellebroussardphoto.com

New Hope Chapel at Noël Acadien au Village, Lafayette

CAJUN COUNTRY
Lake Charles, Lafayette, New Iberia, Houma, Thibodaux

Noël Acadien au Village
Over half a million lights and displays decorate LARC's Acadian Village in Lafayette, a Cajun village created with authentic Creole and Cajun houses. There is musical entertainment each night, local cuisine, photos with Santa and kiddie carnival rides.
www.acadianvillage.org

Hanley-Gueno Neapolitan Presepio
This exhibit of Eighteenth-Century figurines created by Neapolitan craftsmen is one of the largest collections in the country. Display features the Holy Family, Magi and shepherds in the midst of typical street scenes of Eighteenth-Century Italy.
Cathedral of St. John the Evangelist Museum, 515 Cathedral Street, Lafayette; 337-232-1322, www.stjohncathedral.org

Cajun Christmas
Lake Charles celebrates with a month of activities, including ice skating, concerts, theater performances, carriage rides, music, street parade and more. A boat parade showcases a variety of boats decorated with lights and competing for prizes. Fireworks extravaganza over the lake follows the boat parade.
www.visitlakecharles.com

Grevemberg House
Historic Grevemberg House in Franklin is decorated with a Victorian Christmas tree and seasonal greenery.
407 Sterling Rd. (Hwy. 322), ww.grevemberghouse.com

Shadows-on-the-Teche
Daily tours at this historic home feature information on merry-making seasons in the past. Stroll down Main Street to see lights, ancient oaks and beautiful homes. www.shadowsontheteche.wordpress.com

St. Lucy Festival of Lights
St. Lucy is the patron saint of the blind, and her name is derived from the Latin word for light. The St. Lucy Festival includes light displays featuring angels in trees, an outdoor Mass and Christmas parade, as well as live music, arts and crafts, food and activities on the historic St. Martin de Tours Square in St. Martinville. At dusk, beautiful lights are turned on to illuminate the square. 337-394-9404, 337-224-1627, www.cajuncountry.org

Joseph Jefferson Home and Rip Van Winkle Gardens
Take a tour of the Joseph Jefferson home and gardens on Lake Peigneur, and see the house decorated for the holiday season. 5505 Rip Van Winkle Rd., New Iberia; 337-359-5505, www.ripvanwinklegardens.com

Christmas Boat Parade
Celebrate Christmas along the waterside in the town of Delcambre. See shrimp boats up close and boats of all sizes decked out with lights and holiday colors. There is an abundance of toe-tapping music, entertainment, fireworks and food. 337-349-0229, www.delcambreboatparade.com

Le Grand Noël
Enjoy an evening of shopping, carriage rides and food in the Grand Coteau historic district, listed on the National Register of Historic Places and home of the Academy of the Sacred Heart. www.grandcoteau.org, www.lafayettetravel.com

A Bayou Christmas

Pageantry, Santa, Santa's workshop and sleigh rides through the park highlight this annual festival, which is held at Larose Civic Center in Larose. www.visitlafourche.com, www.bayoucivicclub.org

Grant Christmas Tree Farm and Syrup Mill

On three Saturdays following Thanksgiving, the farm plans special activities to coincide with selecting and cutting a tree. See syrup being made the old-fashioned way with a donkey and a cane press, and watch the juice boiling over a fire. Activities include food, bluegrass and gospel music, a petting zoo, hayrides and arts and crafts. 800-987-NOEL, www.grantchristmastreefarm.com

Old Time Christmas at Vermilionville

This historic Cajun village celebrates Christmas from days past. Learn about holiday traditions and activities from French Louisiana in the 17th and 18th centuries. www.vermilionville.org

Christmas in Old Opelousas

Celebrate in Louisiana's third oldest city. The month-long celebration includes lighting events, music, activities and a life-size Nativity scene. www.cityofopelousas.com

Christmas Under the Oaks

Visit Sulphur to see ancient oaks decked out with lights and snowflakes. Activities include carnival rides, Spectacle of Lights, entertainment and the Balloon Parade. Event takes place at the Brimstone Museum Complex in Heritage Square. www.visitlakecharles.org

Chewy Plantation Pie, Desserts, page 144

LOUISIANA CUISINE

Louisiana cuisine is as diverse as the recipes for jambalaya. In the south from New Orleans to Lafayette, Cajun and Creole cuisine is renowned, recognized throughout the world for its unique blend of spices and flavors. In North Louisiana, nothing can beat the satisfying comfort of country home cooking and soul food. With a rich heritage from French, Spanish, African, Native American, Caribbean, Acadian, German, English and Italian cultures, Louisiana offers something for every taste. Delectable flavors in holiday recipes come from the spices and bounty of farmlands, and coastal waters and lakes provide an abundance of seafood and fish. Local produce and Louisiana seafood help create the foundation for memorable and delicious holiday meals.

Bon Appetit!

Hanley-Gueno Neapolitan Presepio; Lafayette, Louisiana

Hors D'Oeuvres

Caprese Salad Skewers

12 cherry tomatoes
6 large marinated black and green olives
6 fresh basil leaves
Fresh mozzarella cheese
Balsamic vinaigrette
Short skewers

Cut mozzarella cheese into one-inch cubes or balls. Thread one tomato, one basil leaf, one olive, cheese and another tomato on each skewer. Put skewers into pan and drizzle balsamic vinaigrette over vegetables and cheese. Makes six. Double or triple recipe, as needed.

➤ *This fresh and easy appetizer is a welcome addition to winter menus.*

Caprese Salad Skewers

Many varieties of fresh herbs can be grown in Louisiana. The LSU AgCenter reports that basil is a warm season annual herb that grows from spring until the first freeze.

Crescent City Oysters

1 pint of oysters with liquid
2 to 3 rounded tablespoons flour
3 to 4 tablespoons oil
1 cup chopped vegetable seasoning blend
1 stalk celery, finely chopped
2 tablespoons parsley, chopped
Salt, pepper and Cajun seasoning
Puff pastry shells or tart shells

Prepare shells or tarts following package directions. Drain oysters and set aside. Reserve liquid. In medium pan, bring oyster liquid (without oysters) to a boil. Chop oysters, depending on size, and add to liquid. Cook until oysters begin to curl. Remove from heat. Remove oysters from liquid and strain liquid. In a skillet, brown flour in oil. Add chopped seasoning, celery and parsley, along with salt, pepper and Cajun seasoning. Sauté until vegetables wilt. Add liquid from oysters to mixture; heat and stir until thickened. Add oysters, and then distribute mixture evenly into shells. Serve warm.

> ➤ *This is an old New Orleans recipe from the Pfeffer-Constantin family, handed down through three generations. Serve as an appetizer in tart shells or as a first course or side dish in puff pastry shells. The oyster liquor is an important part of the flavor in the dish and is often referred to as the "holy water."*

Gulf coast waters provide 70 percent of the oysters caught in the United States. Louisiana oysters are largest during the cooler months.

Duck and Bacon Bites

4 duck breasts
4 to 6 jalapeno peppers
Seasonings: salt, pepper, thyme, sage
1 (1-pound) package bacon

Remove meat from breastbone and cut into pieces about
1 1/2 inches. Season well with salt, pepper, thyme and
sage. Place a section of jalapeno with each piece of meat,
and wrap with about 1/3 piece of bacon. Secure with
toothpick. Put on grill. When bacon is crisp, it's ready.
May also be baked in oven at 325 degrees F.

> ➤ *The late John Sylvest of New Roads often used a*
> *puddle duck with this recipe. Puddle ducks are shallow*
> *feeders and include mallard, pintail, teal, gadwall and*
> *widgeon.*

Gueydan, the Duck Capital of America, has been
hosting the annual Duck Festival since 1977. The festival
highlights the abundance of waterfowl in the area and
the hunting heritage of Louisiana. Activities include
Duck and Goose Calling Contests, Decoy Carving, great
food and music.

Southern Sausage Balls

1 pound bulk sausage, hot or regular
4 cups shredded cheese
3 cups biscuit mix
1/4 cup finely chopped celery (optional)
1/4 cup finely chopped green onion (optional)
1 egg, lightly beaten
1 tablespoon melted butter
Hot sauce to taste

Preheat oven to 350 degrees F. In a large skillet, brown the sausage with celery and onion, and drain well. In a large mixing bowl, combine sausage mixture with biscuit mix, egg, cheese, butter and hot sauce (to taste). Mix well. Form into balls (about 1 inch in size). Bake on lightly greased baking sheets for 20 to 25 minutes, until lightly browned. Can be made ahead and frozen.

> ➤ *This is one of many versions of the classic sausage ball recipe. Whether using the original recipe with only the first three ingredients (biscuit mix, sausage and cheese) or adding veggies and seasonings, this is a perennial favorite for breakfast or as a snack when watching the game.*

Boudin is a popular Cajun sausage traditionally created from a blend of rice, pork and spices. Crawfish and shrimp boudin with Cajun spices are popular also. Boudin is served everywhere from the fanciest restaurants to country gas stations and is great to serve as an appetizer or side. For a guide to the best boudin in South Louisiana and ideas on serving and heating, visit www.boudinlink.com.

Zesty Sausage Squares
D. K. Crawford, www.thefoodsavant.blogspot.com

1 cup buttermilk biscuit mix
1/3 cup milk
4 tablespoons mayonnaise
1 pound hot bulk sausage
1/2 cup chopped onions
1 egg
2 cups grated cheddar cheese
2 cans chopped green chilies

Preheat oven to 375 degrees F. Mix biscuit mix with milk and 2 tablespoons mayonnaise. Spread in well-greased 9 x 13 inch pan. Pat down. Sauté sausage and onion in frying pan. Drain. Spread on biscuit mix. Beat egg, two tablespoons mayonnaise, cheese and green chilies. Spread on top of meat. Bake 25 minutes. Cut into squares before serving.

> ➤ *D. K. Crawford, a food writer from Lafayette, now living in California, takes this dish when visiting family and friends, because it not only tastes great, but also travels well.*

Hearty Queso Dip

1 pound of ground beef
1 (32-ounce) box Velveeta cheese
1 (16-ounce) jar chili sauce

Brown ground meat in a skillet. Drain and combine with cheese and chili sauce in a crockpot. Serve warm with tortilla chips.

Petite Meatball Appetizers

1 pound ground beef
1 pound ground pork
1 package dry onion soup mix
4 eggs
1/2 cup milk
1 cup seasoned bread crumbs
1 tablespoon Worcestershire Sauce
1 tablespoon Tiger Sauce
Cayenne pepper

Preheat oven to 350 degrees F. Mix beef, pork, onion
soup mix, eggs, milk and bread crumbs in a large bowl.
Season with Worcestershire sauce, Tiger sauce and
cayenne pepper to your taste. Roll mixture into bite-sized
meatballs and brown in the oven about 30 minutes.
Serve with the simple dip that follows.

Appetizer Dip

1 jar Heinz Chili Sauce
1/2 jar or more of grape jelly or other jelly of
        your choice

Mix these two ingredients well, and serve as a dipping
sauce for meatballs.

> ➤ *No time to make meatballs? Substitute Lil' Smokies for
> meatballs, and heat in Appetizer Dip.*

Crab Dip

1/2 stick butter
1 small bunch of green onions, chopped
1/2 cup of fresh parsley, chopped
2 tablespoons flour
1 pint whipping cream
1 tablespoon sherry
1 pound crabmeat
Salt, pepper, hot sauce to taste

Melt butter in heavy pot, and sauté onions and parsley. Blend in flour gradually. Stir in cream. Add sherry, seasonings and crabmeat. Serve warm.

Louisiana leads the nation in production of both hard and soft-shell crabs. Blue crabs are available year round, although more plentiful in warmer months. March is historically the month crabs are least available.

Nina's New Orleans Remoulade Sauce

Nina Piazza Baumer, Paul Piazza & Son
www.paulpiazza.com

1 (32-ounce) jar of Blue Plate Mayonnaise
1 (16-ounce) jar of Zatarain's® Creole Mustard
1/3 cup lemon juice
1 bunch of green onions, chopped
1 bunch of celery, chopped
1 to 2 tablespoons of cayenne pepper for taste
1 to 2 tablespoons of paprika
Ketchup for color, Heinz or Hunts

Mix everything together. One recipe will handle ten pounds of boiled shrimp.

> ➤ *Nina often uses Light Blue Plate Mayonnaise. She makes her sauce very pink, so she uses almost a whole small bottle of ketchup.*

Boiled Shrimp
www.zatarains.com

2 quarts water
2 tablespoons salt (optional)
2 pounds large shrimp with shells (21-30 count)
2 teaspoons Zatarain's® Concentrated Shrimp
    and Crab Boil or 1 package Zatarain's®
    Crawfish, Shrimp and Crab Boil-In a Bag

Bring water and salt to boil in large saucepot. Add shrimp and Crab Boil. Return to boil; cover. Cook 2 minutes or until shrimp turn pink. Remove from heat. Let stand 2 minutes. Drain well.

Crawfish Appetizer

1/2 stick of butter
1 bunch green onions, chopped
2 tablespoons of flour
1 pound of crawfish tails
1 can of sliced mushrooms
Seasonings - salt, red pepper, garlic powder,
      lemon juice, hot sauce to taste
8 ounces sour cream

Melt butter in pan and sauté green onions. Add flour.
Then add crawfish, mushrooms and seasonings to taste.
Cook down for approximately 10 to 15 minutes. Add
sour cream just before serving. Serve as a dip or in puff
pastry shells or tart shells. Fills 12 puff pastries.

Diana's Cheese Log

8 ounces cream cheese
2 cups shredded sharp cheddar cheese
1 tablespoon finely chopped onion
1 tablespoon finely chopped green pepper
1 tablespoon chopped pimento
2 teaspoons Worcestershire sauce
2 teaspoons lemon juice
Red pepper, salt to taste

Soften cream cheese, and mix with shredded cheese.
Add all other ingredients and mix. Shape into a ball or
log. Chill and serve with crackers or toasted bagels.

Smoked Salmon Spread

8 ounces cream cheese, softened
4 ounces smoked salmon, chopped
1/4 cup chopped fresh dill
Hot pepper sauce, optional

In a medium bowl, stir cream cheese until it is no longer in a hard form. Add salmon, dill and hot pepper sauce; mix well. Chill and serve with crackers or bagels.

➢ *Proportion of salmon to cream cheese may vary somewhat.*

Rosemary Olive Cheese Spread
Sarah Liberta, HERBS by Sarah
www.herbsbysarah.com

8 ounces cream cheese, softened
1 tablespoon mixed dried herbs, such as parsley,
        chives, garlic, celery seed
1 teaspoon fresh rosemary, chopped fine
        or 1/3 teaspoon dried, crushed rosemary
1/2 cup pitted ripe olives, chopped
1/2 cup grated Parmesan cheese
2 tablespoons milk

Place all ingredients in bowl of small food processor and pulse until combined. Transfer to small bowl and store covered in refrigerator several hours or overnight so flavors will blend. Serve with crackers or crudités.

Rosemary Walnuts
Sarah Liberta, HERBS by Sarah
www.herbsbysarah.com

2 tablespoons extra virgin olive oil
      or melted butter or margarine
1 tablespoon fresh rosemary
      or 1 teaspoon dried rosemary
1/2 teaspoon salt
1/4 teaspoon cayenne pepper
2 cups walnut halves

Preheat oven to 350 degrees F. Mix oil and seasonings together in a shallow baking pan. Add walnuts and toss to coat. Spread in single layer. Roast in oven about 7 to 10 minutes, until lightly browned, shaking occasionally. Do not over brown or nuts will taste bitter. Nuts will become crisp as they cool.

Rosemary is the herb most often associated with the Christmas holidays. Some say it was one of the manger herbs and that it blooms on Christmas night in celebration of the birth of the Christ child. Another legend says that, on the flight into Egypt, Mary placed her blue cloak over a blooming rosemary bush while bathing the infant Jesus in the river. When she removed her cloak, the white flowers had turned to blue, as they remain to this day.—Sarah Liberta

Hanley-Gueno Neapolitan Presepio; Lafayette, Louisiana

Les Pains

Apple Cranberry Muffins

3 cups shredded, unpeeled red and green apples
1 1/2 cups sugar
1 cup chopped cranberries
1 cup shredded carrots
1 cup chopped pecans or walnuts
1 1/2 cups all-purpose flour
1 tablespoon baking powder
2 teaspoons baking soda
1/2 teaspoon salt
2 teaspoons cinnamon
2 eggs, slightly beaten
1/2 cup vegetable oil

Preheat oven to 375 degrees F. After shredding the apples, squeeze out the excess juice. Mix together apples and sugar in large bowl. Fold in cranberries, carrots and nuts. In small bowl, combine dry ingredients and add to apple mixture. Mix well to moisten. Stir in eggs and oil. Mix well. Fill greased muffin cups 2/3 full. Bake 25 minutes. If using mini muffin pans, bake 12 to 18 minutes. Cool about five minutes before removing from pan. Makes about 18 regular-size muffins.

> ➤ *A delicious and nutritious breakfast muffin for the holidays. From Jenny Wright, Lafayette.*

The Louisiana Pecan Festival is a three-day event held in November each year in Colfax in Grant Parish. Events include pecan-cooking and pie-eating contests, antique tractor show, pageantry, musical entertainment, a parade, fireworks, a Country Store and fun events and activities for all ages.

Pumpkin Bread

3 cups sugar
3 1/2 cups flour
2 teaspoons baking soda
1 teaspoon baking powder
1 teaspoon each nutmeg, cloves, cinnamon,
    allspice, salt
4 eggs
2 cups pumpkin
1 cup cooking oil
1 cup water
1 cup raisins
1 cup nuts

Preheat oven to 325 degrees F. Grease and flour three loaf pans. Mix dry ingredients together in large bowl. Add remaining ingredients and mix well. Bake in loaf pans for 1 hour or until bread tests done when a toothpick is inserted into the center. Makes 15 to 18 mini loaves or 3 mid-size. For mini muffins bake about 15 minutes.

> ➤ *Rosemary Florstedt of Lafayette gives this pumpkin bread to friends during the holidays. It can be served with cream cheese, preserves or Satsuma Honey Butter (p. 172).*

Whole Wheat Banana Nut Bread

1 3/4 cups whole wheat flour
1/2 teaspoon salt
1/3 cup vegetable oil
1/2 cup honey
1 teaspoon vanilla
2 eggs
3 ripe bananas, mashed
1 teaspoon baking soda
1/4 cup hot water
1/2 cup chopped nuts

Preheat oven to 325 degrees F. In a bowl stir flour and salt together. In a mixing bowl beat honey and oil together. Add vanilla, then eggs, one at a time. Mix in bananas. Add baking soda to hot water and stir to mix; add to batter alternately with the flour and salt mixture. Stir in chopped nuts. Pour batter in greased 9 x 5 inch loaf pan. Bake 55 to 60 minutes, or until toothpick inserted into the center comes out clean. Cool on wire rack at least 30 minutes before slicing. Makes 1 large loaf. This recipe may be doubled.

> ➤ *Eating smart can be so delicious. Double the recipe to make tasty gifts. Mini Banana Nut Bread loaves may be made by dividing the batter among four miniature loaf pans and reducing baking time to about 30 minutes.*

Banana plants are grown throughout Louisiana as ornamental shrubs. According to LSU AgCenter, in areas south of I-10 the plants sometimes produce edible fruit, although the raw bananas in the plantain or cooking banana class may not be flavorful.

Stuffed French Toast
Mary Brown, The Cottage Plantation, St. Francisville
www.cottageplantation.com

4 ounces cream cheese, softened
1/4 cup chopped dates
1/4 cup chopped pecans
4 teaspoons orange marmalade
2 French bread loaves, cut diagonally into 2-inch
    slices (about 8 slices)
4 large eggs
1 cup milk
1 teaspoon cinnamon
3 tablespoons butter or margarine

Stir together cream cheese and the next three ingredients. Cut a horizontal pocket into the top of the sliced bread. Spoon about 2 teaspoons of the mixture into each slice. Beat together the eggs, cinnamon and milk. Dip stuffed bread into the mixture, coating on all sides. Melt butter in a large non-stick skillet. Cook the slices about 2 minutes on each side until golden brown. Sprinkle with powdered sugar. Serve with syrup. Makes 8 servings. Recipe can be doubled.

> ➤ *This recipe is a favorite with B&B guests at The Cottage. After a hearty, full plantation breakfast, many guests tour the beautiful grounds and historic home.*

Pain Perdue

6 eggs
1 1/2 cups milk
1 to 2 teaspoons of sugar
Dash of salt
1 teaspoon vanilla
1 teaspoon nutmeg
1 teaspoon cinnamon
1/2 stick butter
1/2 loaf of bread
Confectioner's sugar

In a wide bowl, beat eggs. Add salt, milk, sugar, vanilla, nutmeg and cinnamon. Stir mixture well. Begin melting butter in a skillet; dip each slice of bread into the egg mixture on both sides, allowing bread to soak up the mixture. Soak several pieces at a time; then put into a skillet and brown on each side. Continue the process with each piece of bread. Sprinkle confectioner's sugar over each piece of toast or serve with syrup.

Sicily Island Hotcakes

2 eggs
2 cups buttermilk
Pinch of salt
1/2 teaspoon baking soda
2 tablespoons sugar
2 teaspoons baking powder
2 to 3 cups all-purpose flour

Beat eggs. Add buttermilk. Add soda, sugar, salt and baking powder. Gradually add flour to thicken mixture to the right consistency for pancakes. Heat griddle or pan. Add butter, and when it's sizzling (be careful not to burn), pour in about 1/4 to 1/2 cup pancake mixture. Cook on one side until bubbles begin to form on top, and then flip and continue cooking on the other side.

➢ *Whether you call them hotcakes or pancakes, everyone loves them. The late Barnie Lee Stubbs of Sicily Island, Louisiana, used this recipe to cook hotcakes on a small cast iron griddle with lots of butter. She could cook only two at a time, but they were worth the wait. Make the batter up to a day ahead and refrigerate until ready to use.*

The traditional kick-off of syrup-making season for Steen's Syrup Mill in Abbeville was the sound of the steam whistle. Mr. C.F. Steen began making syrup in 1910 to save his frozen crop of sugar cane. Traditionally, the syrup-making season is from October through Christmas.

Coffee Lovers' Coffee Cake

2 cups all-purpose flour
2 teaspoons instant coffee granules
2 cups firmly packed light brown sugar
1 teaspoon ground cinnamon
1/2 teaspoon salt
1/2 cup butter, cut into pieces
1 (8-ounce) carton sour cream
1 teaspoon baking soda
1 large egg, beaten
1/4 cup chopped pecans or walnuts

Preheat oven to 350 degrees F. Combine flour and coffee granules in a large bowl. Add brown sugar, cinnamon and salt; stir well. Cut in butter with a pastry blender until crumbly. Press half of crumb mixture into a greased 9 inch square pan; set aside. Combine sour cream and baking soda, stirring well. Add to remaining crumb mixture, stirring just until dry ingredients are moistened. Add egg, stirring gently to combine. Pour sour cream mixture over crumb crust in pan; sprinkle with pecans. Bake for 45 minutes.

Coffee is the drink of choice throughout Louisiana, and the darker the roast, the better. Coffee came to North America by way of New Orleans. Chicory was added during times when coffee beans were scarce, but it has become a flavor preferred by many.

Almond Biscotti

2 cups unbleached flour
1 teaspoon baking powder
1/4 teaspoon salt
4 tablespoons butter
1 cup sugar
2 large eggs
1/2 teaspoon vanilla extract
1/4 teaspoon almond extract
3/4 cup whole almonds with skin
2 teaspoons orange zest
       or 1/2 teaspoon orange oil

Preheat oven to 350 degrees F. Toast almonds on cookie sheet in oven for 8 to 10 minutes. Cool. Cover almonds with a clean dishtowel or put in freezer bag, and crush with a meat tenderizer. Set aside. Sift together flour, baking powder and salt, and set aside. Mix together butter and sugar until well blended. Add in eggs, vanilla and almond extracts, crushed almonds and orange zest. Mix in flour and stir everything together with a wooden spoon. Coat hands with flour and fold and knead dough to blend. Shape into a long loaf about 4 x 12 inches. Place on lightly greased baking pan or use parchment paper. Bake on middle rack in oven for 30 minutes. Cool for 10 minutes. Lower temperature to 325 degrees F. Slice loaf, and then bake for 10 to 15 minutes or more depending on how dry or crisp you want the biscotti to be. Cool completely and store tightly covered.

> ➢ *Keep biscotti on hand during the holidays. Store in a jar on the counter, and let everyone help themselves. Great for breakfast or as a snack.*

Jalapeno Cornbread

3 jalapeno peppers (may use fewer)
3 eggs
3 cups corn meal mix
3 cups grated mild cheese
2 1/2 cups milk
1 large onion, finely chopped
1/2 cup salad oil
1 can of cream-style corn

Preheat oven to 350 degrees F. Mix everything together. Bake at 350 degrees in a 13 x 9 inch pan about 35 minutes. Makes 10 to 12 servings.

Crispy French Bread

1 day-old baguette or French bread loaf
1 stick butter, softened
Garlic powder

Preheat oven to 400 degrees F. Slice stale bread in thin (1/8 to 1/4 inch slices). For easier cutting, use an electric knife. Spread each piece on both sides with butter and sprinkle with garlic powder. Stand up bread slices in 9 x 13 inch pan. Put pan in hot oven for about 15 minutes, reduce heat to 250 degrees F. and leave in oven for 2 hours or until bread is crispy. Cool and store in airtight container.

> ➤ *This recipe from the late Betty Jean Tompkins of Lafayette is great to make ahead and have on hand for meals. It's good as a snack or with dips and spreads.*

Bacon Cheddar Muffins
Blake Payne, Pastry Chef
Cypress Bayou Casino, Charenton

1 cup vegetable oil
1 1/2 cups milk
2 whole eggs
1 small can cream of mushroom soup
2 teaspoons salt
1 tablespoon sugar
1 tablespoon garlic powder
1/2 cup grated Parmesan cheese
1 cup grated cheddar cheese
1/4 cup sliced green onions
3 cups flour
2 tablespoons baking powder
1/2 cup chopped cooked bacon

Preheat oven to 350 degrees F. Mix together oil, milk, eggs, soup, salt and sugar. Mix for 3 minutes on medium speed. Then add garlic powder, both cheeses and onions. Mix for another 3 minutes. Combine baking powder with flour and add to the mixture and mix for 2 minutes. Fold in bacon bits last. Scoop batter into a muffin pan that is non-stick and bake in a 350 degree oven for about 40 minutes or until a toothpick comes out clean. Makes 16 muffins.

Christmas Morning Sausage Rolls
Jeremy Conner, Chef de Cuisine
Village Café, Lafayette

2 premade pie crusts
Jimmy Dean fresh sausage
All-purpose flour

Sprinkle a clean flat work surface with flour and place pie crusts flat on surface side by side so that they just overlap. Sprinkle top of crusts with more flour. With rolling pin, roll crusts together and into a rectangle shape about 20 inches on the top and bottom and 10 to 12 inches on the sides. With fingers, spread sausage evenly over surface of crusts. Gently pull one edge of the crust free from the work surface and roll it all tightly into a log shape. Refrigerate or freeze until ready to use.

15 minutes before ready to bake, preheat oven to 350 degrees F. If roll is in freezer, place in refrigerator, and vice versa. The temperature between frozen and refrigerated is the optimum for slicing the roll. When ready to bake, slice the roll crosswise about 3/8 inch thick and place slices on a greased cookie sheet. Bake for about ten minutes or until crispy and golden brown.

➢ *My family makes these a few days before Christmas, and we always make extra to give to friends and neighbors so they can also enjoy them on Christmas morning. They are great with the first cup of coffee and will get you through until time for the real breakfast.–Jeremy Connor*

Deer Sausage Braids

1 pound bulk sausage (can be deer, beef, turkey
    or pork)
Salt and pepper to taste
1 cup chopped scallions
1 (8-ounce) package cream cheese
1/2 cup red or yellow bell pepper, chopped
1 (8-ounce) package ready-to-bake crescent roll
    dough

Preheat oven to 350 degrees F. Brown meat and add
next four ingredients. Cook and stir until the cream
cheese melts; allow it to cool. Roll out dough (I press it
on a non-stick surface) into a 12 x 8 inch rectangle
sealing the perforations to make a solid sheet of dough.
Spoon cooled meat mixture into the center of the dough
and make diagonal slices into the dough on both sides of
the mixture. Fold the ends of the dough over the meat,
and alternately braid the slits across the mixture. Brush
with egg wash (1 egg beaten with 1 teaspoon water) and
bake at 350 degrees for about 15 minutes or until golden
brown. The braids freeze well (after baked), and the
recipe can be used to make as many as you wish.

> *Mary Elizabeth Watson comes from a family of hunters.
> She has created many of her own recipes using a variety of
> meat from the great outdoors.*

Sausage Bread

3 loaves frozen bread dough, thawed
1 1/2 pounds bulk sausage—mild or hot
     depending on taste
1 cup chopped vegetable seasoning blend
Salt and pepper to taste
2 eggs, slightly beaten
1 to 2 cups shredded cheese (mozzarella and/or
     cheddar and Monterrey Jack

Preheat oven to 350 degrees F. In skillet, brown sausage
and vegetables. Drain. Let cool slightly. In large mixing
bowl, combine salt, pepper, eggs and cheese. Add
sausage. Roll out bread dough in rectangle. Spread
sausage mixture on each loaf, leaving about a one-inch
border. Roll up lengthwise and seal edges—use a little
water if needed. Spray cookie sheet with non-stick
cooking spray. Move loaf to cookie sheet. Cut slits on
top of loaf in several places to allow steam to vent. Let
bread rise about 35 minutes—not double. Bake for 25 to
35 minutes or until golden brown. Freezes well.

The German tradition of sausage making was brought to
Louisiana in the 1700s. Like many other things in the
French-speaking region of the country, it was given a
French name, Andouille. At that time most of the
Andouille was made at the boucherie during winter.

Make-Ahead Breakfast Casserole

8 ounces cubed stuffing mix or 6 to 8 slices bread
torn into pieces
12 ounces shredded cheddar-jack cheese
1 (4-ounce) can diced green chilies
2 1/2 cups milk
6 eggs
1 can cream of mushroom soup

Spray 9 x 13 inch pan with nonstick spray. Cover
bottom of pan with stuffing mix or bread pieces.
Sprinkle cheese over stuffing. Beat the remaining
ingredients together and pour over stuffing and cheese.
Cover and put in refrigerator overnight. Bake at 350
degrees F for approximately 1 hour or until firm and not
overly brown. Allow to sit for 5 minutes before serving.
Serves 8.

Artichoke Bread

1/2 to 3/4 cups mayonnaise
1 cup freshly grated Parmesan cheese
1 can artichoke hearts, chopped
2 teaspoons garlic
1 loaf French bread, split in half
Chopped green onions or parsley for garnish

Preheat oven to 325 degrees F. Mix together
mayonnaise, cheese, artichoke hearts and garlic. Spread
mixture on each half of bread. Bake until golden brown.
Garnish before serving.

➤   *This bread recipe from Nancy Chustz of New Roads is good as*
   an appetizer or a side dish.

No-Knead Wheat Rolls

1 1/4 cups all-purpose or unbleached flour
1 cup whole wheat flour
1 teaspoon salt
2 tablespoons sugar
1 package yeast
1 cup water (120 to 150 degrees F)
2 tablespoons butter, melted
1 egg

Mix 3/4 cup white flour, 1/2 cup whole wheat flour, salt, sugar and yeast. Stir in the water, butter and egg, and beat with the spoon until well mixed and smooth. Add enough of the remaining flours to form a soft dough. Cover the bowl and put it in a warm place to rise. Let it rise about 30 minutes or until double in size. While it is rising, grease a regular muffin pan with butter. After it has risen, beat the dough about 25 strokes with a spoon. Then spoon the dough into the muffin pan. Cover again, and let it rise about 30 minutes or until the dough rises out of the muffin holders. Preheat the oven to 400 degrees F. Bake about 15 to 20 minutes or until brown.

➤ *The smell of home-baked bread is especially welcoming during the holidays.*

Hanley-Gueno Neapolitan Presepio; Lafayette, Louisiana

Les Salades et Les Soupes

Fresh Cranberry Relish

2 oranges
4 cups raw cranberries
2 cups sugar
1 ounce brandy, or less (optional)
1 cup chopped, toasted pecans

Preheat oven to 350 degrees F. Peel oranges and remove seeds and white membrane. Put oranges and cranberries into food processor and pulse until chopped—not pulverized. Place chopped ingredients into medium size bowl and stir in sugar and brandy. Mix well to blend. Toast chopped pecans on cookie sheet in preheated oven for about 5 minutes—check and be careful they do not burn. Add to relish mixture and refrigerate until ready to serve.

Instant Cranberry Relish

1 can whole-berry cranberry sauce
1/2 cup chopped pecans
1 to 2 satsumas or 1 orange, chopped

Gently toss all the ingredients together and chill for several hours or until time to serve.

Southern Ambrosia

1 cup fresh coconut, grated
1 cup chopped pecans or walnuts
1 grapefruit, peeled and sectioned
2 oranges, peeled and sectioned
2 (8-ounce) cans pineapple chunks
1/4 to 1/2 cup orange juice

Preheat oven to 350 degrees F. Toast nuts and coconut for five to eight minutes. Peel fruit and remove white membranes. Cut fruit sections in half. In bowl, layer grapefruit, then pineapple, then orange and sprinkle with coconut and nuts. Repeat layers. Pour orange juice over layers.

> ➤ *Ambrosia is a popular salad, particularly in the South. It is typically mixed with whipped cream, sour cream or marshmallows. This recipe, a variation on the old Southern classic, calls for only the fruit, sweetened with orange juice. It makes a beautiful and fresh salad to serve during the holidays.*

Olive Citrus Salad

Lettuce, mix of romaine and iceberg
3 tablespoons white wine vinegar
2 tablespoons vegetable oil
3 tablespoons honey
1/4 teaspoon basil
1/2 teaspoon dried rosemary leaves
1/4 teaspoon pepper
Salt to taste
1 1/2 cups ripe pitted black olives
1/2 cup slivered almonds
1/2 medium red onion, thinly sliced
3 oranges, peeled and sectioned

Make the dressing ahead. Combine oil, vinegar, honey, basil, rosemary, pepper and salt. Add olives to the dressing, and refrigerate 6 to 8 hours or overnight. To serve salad, mix lettuces, onions, nuts and oranges. Toss with dressing. Makes 6 to 8 servings.

> ➤ *This delicious salad takes advantage of fresh Louisiana oranges. Recipe is from Ann Palombo of Lafayette.*

December is peak season for Louisiana citrus. Many of the state's citrus growers sell directly to the public at farmers' markets and roadside stands.

Broccoli Salad

1 head broccoli
8 ounces cheddar cheese
1/2 small red onion, chopped
1 cup golden raisins
1 cup salted peanuts
1 cup red grapes
1/2 to 1 cup mayonnaise
2 tablespoons sugar
1 1/2 tablespoons red wine vinegar
Salt and pepper, to taste

Wash the broccoli head and remove the large leaves and tough stalk. Cut the head into flowerets and the tender stem into small pieces. Cut the cheese into bite-size cubes. Put the broccoli, raisins, onion, peanuts, cheese and grapes in a large bowl. In a separate container, mix the mayonnaise, vinegar, seasonings and sugar until well blended. Add to the ingredients in the large bowl.

Festive Pistachio Salad

3 (1/2-ounce) box instant pistachio pudding
1 (8-ounce) carton of Cool Whip
2 cups miniature marshmallows
1/2 cup chopped pecans
1 (20-ounce) can crushed pineapple
Small jar of cherries, optional

Mix pudding and Cool Whip well. Add pecans and marshmallows slowly. Then add the pineapple. Mix well. Refrigerate.

Spicy Louisiana Cole Slaw

Dressing

5 heaping tablespoons mayonnaise
2 heaping tablespoons yellow mustard
2 tablespoons olive oil
1 teaspoon Louisiana hot sauce
2 tablespoons catsup
1/2 to 1 teaspoon garlic salt
1 tablespoon wine vinegar
Juice of 1 medium-size lemon
1 tablespoon Worcestershire sauce
3 teaspoons salt or to taste

Put mayonnaise and mustard in mixing bowl and beat until well combined. Slowly add olive oil, mixing well. Add remaining dressing ingredients and mix well.

Greens

1 to 2 bell peppers, sliced or chopped
1 medium onion, shredded
1 large head of cabbage, shredded

Place cabbage, pepper and onions in large salad bowl. Pour dressing over greens and toss well. Chill for an hour or more before serving.

Garden Pasta Salad

4 ounces dried pasta, such as bowtie or penne
1 cup mayonnaise or creamy dressing
2 tablespoons chopped green onions
1 tablespoon lemon juice
1 tablespoon dried basil
1/2 teaspoon salt
1/2 teaspoon pepper
1 (16-ounce) can chopped green beans
1 1/2 cups of chopped cucumber (seeded)
1 cup finely chopped carrots
1 cup thinly sliced zucchini
1 cup thinly sliced radishes
1/2 cup chopped bell peppers

Cook the pasta until tender, following directions on package. In a large bowl, stir together the mayonnaise, onions, lemon juice, basil, salt and pepper until smooth. Drain green beans. Add pasta, green beans and remaining ingredients to bowl; toss to coat well. Cover and chill. Makes 8 servings.

Bean Salad

1 bunch green onions, sliced
1 bell pepper, chopped
2 cans cut green beans, drained
1 can cut wax beans, drained
1 can black beans, drained and rinsed
Cherry tomatoes, optional

Combine ingredients in a large bowl. Add dressing below, and stir well. Chill overnight.

Dressing

2/3 cup vinegar
2/3 cup sugar
1/3 cup salad oil
1 1/2 teaspoons salt
1 teaspoon pepper

Stir ingredients until well mixed and pour over the vegetables.

> ➤ *Using red, yellow or orange bell peppers makes the salad more colorful.*

German Potato Salad

6 medium potatoes, sliced
6 strips bacon
1 bunch green onions, chopped
2 tablespoons flour
1/2 cup water
1/3 cup vinegar
3 tablespoons sugar
1/4 teaspoon pepper
Salt, to taste
1/2 cup chopped parsley (optional)

Cook potatoes in boiling salted water until tender, but not too soft, about 10 minutes. While the potatoes are cooking, fry the bacon in a deep skillet until crisp. Remove and drain on a paper towel. Crumble the drained bacon. Drain as much grease as possible from the skillet. Add the onion and cook 2 to 3 minutes. Add the flour and stir until the onions are coated. Add the water, vinegar, sugar and pepper. Cook until slightly thick. Drain the potatoes and season with salt and pepper. Add the potatoes, bacon and parsley to the skillet. Stir gently until the potatoes are coated and the ingredients are blended. Serve warm. Makes 6 to 8 servings.

German families were among Louisiana's earliest settlers. By 1722, soon after New Orleans was founded, Germans began settling in what is now St. Charles and St. John the Baptist parishes. The coastline in that region was called Cote des Allemands, or the German Coast.

Crowley Rice Salad

2 cups rice
1 cup chicken broth
2 cups water
1/3 cup mayonnaise
1 jar marinated artichoke hearts
2 teaspoons Worcestershire sauce
1/4 teaspoon marjoram
Salt, red pepper, black pepper
1/2 cup chopped bell pepper
8 large stuffed green olives
Green onions, chopped

Cook rice following the directions on the package, substituting 1 cup of chicken broth for 1 cup of water. Cut olives into four slices each. Drain artichoke hearts and reserve liquid. Cut into bite-size pieces. Mix mayonnaise with artichoke marinade until a liquid. Add Worcestershire sauce, marjoram, salt, dash of red pepper and black pepper to liquid. Toss the bell pepper, olives, green onions, artichoke hearts in 1/2 the sauce. Add mixture to cooked rice. Reserve remaining sauce to serve on the side. Serve warm or cold.

One of the oldest festivals in Louisiana, the International Rice Festival, is held each October in Crowley. Events include demonstrations of old-time rice threshing, an Acadian accordion contest, fiddle contest, a 5K run and a car show.

Mary Kate's Cherry Salad
D. K. Crawford, www.thefoodsavant.blogspot.com

1 large can dark sweet cherries
Enough pecan halves to stuff each cherry
1 cup cherry juice (from can)
1 packet unflavored gelatin
1/2 cup cold water
2 tablespoons sherry
Juice of 1/2 fresh lemon

Use gelatin mold or bowl for this dish. Lightly oil mold.
Stuff each cherry with one pecan half. Boil juice from
can of cherries and dissolve 1 packet of gelatin in half
cup cold water. Add cherry juice and lemon juice. When
almost cool, add sherry. Place stuffed cherries in mold
and then pour the liquid over them. Refrigerate until
firm. For a special touch, serve with a dollop of crème
fraiche and a hint of freshly cracked pepper.

> ➤ *Mary Kate Wells and my grandmother had coffee
> together every afternoon. Mary Kate's family served as
> missionaries in China, and she and my grandmother
> were inseparable. My first two names come from a
> combination of theirs. This is a festive salad. It's a
> little bit of trouble to stuff the cherries, but it's one of
> my family's all-time holiday favorites.–D. K. Crawford*

D.H. Holmes Chicken Salad

4 to 5 cups cooked chicken, cut in large pieces
2 stalks celery, coarsely chopped
2 green onions, finely chopped
1 tablespoon parsley, chopped
1 apple, peeled and finely chopped
Lemon juice
1/2 cup mayonnaise
1 teaspoon curry powder
Salt and black pepper to taste

Combine chicken in a bowl with celery, onions and parsley. Place chopped apple in small bowl and toss with lemon juice. Stir apple into chicken mixture. In a small bowl, combine mayonnaise and curry powder and blend well. Add to salad and mix together. Add salt and pepper to taste. Chill and serve over lettuce. Makes 4 generous servings.

D.H. Holmes was a department store on Canal Street in New Orleans in the early to late 1900s. The store was known by the large clock on the front of the building, which made it an easily visible and popular place for people to meet. The store had a restaurant that served a chicken salad similar to this one. D.H. Holmes closed in 1989, and the building is now a hotel.

Italian-Style Chicken Salad

3 cups cooked, chopped chicken or turkey
18 ounces Italian dressing
1 cup chopped celery
1 tomato, chopped
16 ounces marinated artichoke hearts, drained
1 (3 1/2-ounce) can sliced black olives
1 head lettuce

In large bowl, combine first six ingredients. Chill until ready to serve. Serve in lettuce lined bowls.

Christmas Chicken Salad

2 cups diced cooked chicken or turkey
1 rib celery, diced
1/4 cup pecan pieces
1/2 cup mayonnaise
1/4 cup sweetened dried cranberries

Combine all ingredients in a bowl. Mix well and chill. Recipe can be doubled.

Dubach is a small town in North Louisiana. Every year the town honors poultry farmers at the Chicken Festival held in September.

Cream of Tomato Soup

1 bunch green onions with tops, chopped
2 tablespoons butter
2 tablespoons flour
Season to taste with salt, pepper and basil
1/2 tablespoon sugar
1 can beef broth (10 1/2 ounces)
1 cup half and half
2 (28-ounce cans) whole tomatoes

Sauté onions in butter in large pot until limp. Add flour and seasonings, blending well. Add sugar, broth and half and half. Heat slowly, blending constantly until smooth and creamy. Put tomatoes, with liquid, in blender and puree. Add tomato puree to pot and simmer 15 to 20 minutes. Do not boil. Garnish with basil.

➤ *A hearty and delicious soup, from Marcia Pickard, formerly of Lafayette.*

BASIL

In 2003 the Creole tomato became the official Louisiana vegetable. It can be grown only in certain parts of south Louisiana.

Roasted Root Vegetable Soup
Anne Patin, Caterer and Cooking Instructor, Lafayette

1 pound carrots, peeled
2 onions, peeled and quartered
1 pound beets, peeled
1 small buttermilk squash, peeled
1 sweet potato, peeled
Olive oil, salt and pepper to taste
1 to 2 quarts of chicken stock

Preheat oven to 425 degrees F. Cut carrots, beets, sweet potato and squash into 1-inch cubes (cut them the same size so vegetables cook evenly). Using two cookie sheets, place vegetables in a single layer and drizzle them with olive oil, salt and pepper. Bake for 25 minutes or until vegetables are tender. Using a spatula, toss once during baking. Test tenderness with a fork. At this point, you can serve roasted vegetables as a side dish. To make soup, place 2 to 3 cups of roasted vegetables in a blender. Gradually add 1 to 2 cups of broth until the soup is the consistency you want. For a smooth purée, add more broth and blend longer. Repeat process until you have used all vegetables. Pour soup back in pot to reheat. Season to taste. Be careful not to over salt. Since roasting enhances the flavor of vegetables, you will be pleased at how dense the flavor is and how sweet this soup is. I have also added turnips and parsnips. The beets make the soup red, which is lovely on a Christmas dinner table. This soup freezes very well.

> ➤ *This is not your typical vegetable soup. It is a purée of roasted winter vegetables and is very sweet, low in calories and high in fiber, and it is a favorite of our family and friends.–Anne Patin*

Green Gumbo (aka Gumbo z'Herbes)
The Saint Street Inn, Lafayette
www.saintstreetinn.com

1 large onion, chopped
1 bell pepper, chopped
1 celery stalk, chopped
1/4 cup garlic, chopped
1/2 cup green onions, chopped
1 carrot, peeled and chopped
3 medium turnips, peeled and chopped
1/2 pound fresh mustard greens, washed and
        chopped
1/2 pound spinach, chopped
1/4 head of cabbage, chopped
1 bunch watercress, chopped
2 quarts vegetable stock
1 can great northern white beans
1 teaspoon thyme
1 bay leaf
1/4 cup parsley, chopped
Salt and cayenne pepper to taste
1 tablespoon olive oil

Heat one tablespoon of olive oil in large pot. Add onion,
bell pepper and celery. Cook until tender. Add turnips,
carrot and garlic. Add greens to pot with 1 quart of stock
and one cup of water. Bring to a boil and simmer over
medium heat until greens are completely wilted. Add
another cup of water along with white beans and
remaining stock and season with salt, pepper, thyme, bay
leaf and watercress. Bring to a boil and reduce to simmer
for about two hours. Season to taste with salt, black
pepper and cayenne. Finish with green onions and
parsley. Serve green or add crispy sautéed sausage.

> While we listed half a dozen domestic greens, the field is wide open, from dandelion greens to pokeweed. According to Leah Chase, the grand dame of Creole cooking, the more different greens you add to the pot, the more friends you'll make over a bowl of soup. We say amen to that.–Nathan Stubbs and Mary Tutwiler, The Saint Street Inn

Farmers' Market Bean Soup

2 cups dried beans, any assortment
Ham bone and trimmings
1 can tomatoes (about 14.5 ounces)
1 (6-ounce) can tomato paste
1 large onion, chopped
1 clove garlic
1 teaspoon chili powder
Salt, pepper and Tony Chachere's to taste
2 bay leaves (optional)

Wash bean mix and soak in water to cover for 3 hours or overnight. Drain. Put 3 quarts of water in stock pot and add other ingredients. Boil slowly 2 1/2 to 3 hours. Remove bay leaves and bone before serving.

> This delicious bean soup recipe from Fran McBride of Welsh is a wonderful way to use leftover holiday ham.

Turkey, Oyster and Smoked Sausage Gumbo

Chef John Folse, John Folse & Company, Gonzales
www.jfolse.com

4 cups turkey meat
1 pint oysters, with liquid
1 pound smoked sausage, sliced
1 cup vegetable oil
1 cup flour
1 cup chopped onions
1 cup chopped celery
1/2 cup chopped green bell peppers
1/4 cup minced garlic
3 quarts water or turkey stock
2 cups sliced green onions
1/2 cup chopped parsley
Salt and cracked black pepper to taste
Granulated garlic to taste
1 tablespoon filé

In a large cast iron pot, heat vegetable oil over medium-high heat. Whisk in flour, stirring constantly until a dark brown roux is achieved. Add onions, celery, bell peppers and minced garlic and sauté 3 to 5 minutes or until vegetables are wilted. Add stock, one ladle at a time, stirring until all is incorporated. Add turkey and smoked sausage and bring to a boil. Reduce heat and simmer 1 to 1 1/2 hours, stirring occasionally. Add oysters, green onions and parsley. Season to taste with salt, pepper and granulated garlic. Cook an additional 5 minutes or until oysters begin to curl. Add filé and serve over steamed white rice. Makes 6 servings.

➤ *This gumbo is perfect after Thanksgiving! The turkey can be taken from leftovers remaining from holiday dinners. May substitute chicken or any other fowl.*

Game Day Chili

4 tablespoons butter
1 onion, diced
2 pounds ground chuck
2 cloves garlic, chopped finely
1 jalapeno pepper, chopped
1 (28-ounce) can crushed tomatoes
1/2 teaspoon cayenne pepper
1 (16-ounce) can enchilada sauce, green or red
3 teaspoons chili powder
1 1/2 to 2 tablespoons salt
1 to 2 tablespoons pepper
3 teaspoons cumin seeds
1 can pinto beans (optional)

Sauté onions in butter until tender. Add garlic and ground meat and brown with onions. Add remaining ingredients. If chili is too thick, thin with heated water. Simmer for two hours. Serves 4, but recipe can easily be doubled. This recipe also freezes well.

➤ *Serve with bowls of chopped onions, grated cheese, Fritos, chopped tomatoes and other extras to let guests create their own special bowl of chili.*

Chili is a southern favorite, particularly during football season. There are many varieties, and cooks pride themselves on adding secret ingredients to make their chili unique. The Louisiana State Chili Cook-Off is held each spring in Baton Rouge.

Easy Crawfish Corn Chowder

1/2 onion, chopped
1/2 bell pepper, chopped
1 clove garlic, minced
1 stick butter
2 cans cream of potato soup
1 can creamed corn
1 can kernel corn
1 pound Louisiana crawfish (or crab or shrimp)
1 quart milk or half and half

Sauté onion, bell pepper and garlic in butter in large saucepan until vegetables are soft. Add crawfish, kernel corn, creamed corn, soup and milk. Stir and cook for 20 to 30 minutes, but do not boil.

The Atchafalaya Basin between Lafayette and Baton Rouge is the world's largest freshwater river basin. Crawfish thrive in freshwater, and about half of the 100 million pounds of crawfish produced in Louisiana each year comes from the basin. The rest come from aquaculture involving 135,000 acres of ponds throughout the state. Breaux Bridge is known as the Crawfish Capital of the World and home of the Breaux Bridge Crawfish Festival, a festival which draws people from around the world. It is held in May each year.

Hanley-Gueno Neapolitan Presepio; Lafayette, Louisiana

Les Légumes et Les Accompagnements

Spinach Madeleine
Anne Patin, Caterer and Cooking Instructor, Lafayette

1 package frozen chopped spinach
2 tablespoons butter
1 tablespoon flour
1 tablespoon finely chopped onion
1/4 cup evaporated milk
Salt and pepper to taste
3 ounces Mexican Velveeta cheese
1/2 teaspoon Worcestershire sauce

Preheat oven to 350 degrees F. Thaw spinach and squeeze dry, setting aside 1/4 cup liquid. In small pan, melt butter. Add flour and stir to form a white roux. Add onion and cook until soft and then gradually add in milk and stir until smooth. Season with salt, pepper and cayenne pepper, if desired. Cut up cheese and add to mixture and stir until melted. Add in Worcestershire sauce. Fold in spinach and mix well. Add spinach liquid if mixture is too thick. Put in small casserole and heat in oven for 15 to 20 minutes. Serves 4. Recipe can be doubled.

> ➢ *This is a rich dish that can be served as a side or as a dip.*

Spinach Madeleine is a very popular holiday dish in Louisiana. The recipe may have originated in St. Francisville or Baton Rouge.

Easy Spinach Casserole

1 (12-ounce) package frozen chopped spinach
3 beaten eggs
6 tablespoons flour
1/2 cup bell pepper, chopped
1 clove garlic, chopped
1 cup onion, chopped
16 ounces small curd cottage cheese
2 cups grated cheddar cheese
1 teaspoon salt
Pepper to taste

Preheat oven to 350 degrees F. In medium mixing bowl beat eggs and flour with fork until smooth. Add cottage cheese. Sauté onion, bell pepper and garlic in oil until wilted and add to cottage cheese and eggs. Add cheddar cheese and seasonings. Bake uncovered in lightly greased 2-quart casserole dish for 35 to 40 minutes or until knife inserted in center comes out clean. Let stand about five minutes before cutting into squares.

> ➤ *Change the flavor of this dish by changing seasonings or cheese: for a Greek flavor, use Feta cheese; for Italian, use Parmesan; for smoky flavor, use provolone.*

According to the LSU AgCenter, more than 40 parishes grow greens to sell. Louisiana greens are sold in farmers' markets, roadside stands and grocery stores. October to May is the best time to find locally-grown greens. The most popular greens grown in Louisiana include mustard greens, turnip greens, collard greens, spinach, kale and Swiss chard.

Cajun Maque Choux
Chef Damon Schexnayder

1/4 cup vegetable oil
1/2 pound Tasso, diced
2 cups onions, diced
1/8 cup minced garlic
1 can Rotel tomatoes, drained
1 cup chicken stock
2 1/2 cups whole kernel corn
1/8 pound unsalted butter
1/4 cup heavy cream
1/8 cup parsley, chopped
1/8 cup green onions, sliced thin
2 tablespoons Louisiana Hot Sauce
Salt and pepper to taste

Using a 6-quart stock pot on medium-high heat, add oil and Tasso. Cook for 5 minutes. Add onions, and cook 5 to 8 minutes, or until translucent. Lower heat to medium. Add Rotel and garlic, and simmer 5 to 6 minutes. Add stock and corn. Cook for 8 minutes or until the corn is soft. Remove from heat. Add cream, butter, parsley, green onions, hot sauce, salt and pepper to taste. Serves 8.

> ➤ *Cajun Maque Choux is a delicious traditional Cajun recipe and the kind of food Damon knows well. When he was only 8 years old, he fell in love with cooking after watching local chefs on LPB create dishes using traditional flavors.*

Jiffy Corn Casserole

1 can whole kernel corn
1 can cream-style corn
1 box Jiffy cornbread mix
2 eggs, beaten
8 ounces sour cream
1/2 stick butter, melted

Preheat oven to 350 degrees F. Combine all ingredients and put in a 9 x 13 inch greased pan. Bake for 45 minutes or until set and lightly browned.

Country Corn Pudding

1 can of cream-style corn
2 tablespoons melted butter
3 eggs, slightly beaten
3 tablespoons flour
1 teaspoon salt
2 tablespoons sugar
1 corn can of milk

Preheat oven to 350 degrees F. Mix all ingredients together and bake in a greased casserole for 45 minutes.

Aw shucks! The Louisiana Corn Festival is held in Bunkie. The summer festival honors corn farmers and features corn shucking and corn eating contests, carnival rides, food vendors and family activities.
www.bunkiechamber.net

Sweet and Sour Green Beans and Carrots

1 cup chopped carrots
3/4 cup water
1 (9-ounce) package frozen cut green beans
2 slices bacon
1 medium onion, coarsely chopped
1 medium apple, peeled or unpeeled
2 tablespoons apple cider vinegar
1 tablespoon sugar
1/4 teaspoon salt

Combine carrots and water in a sauce pan; bring to a boil. Cover, reduce heat and simmer 5 minutes. Add green beans; return to a boil. Cover, reduce heat and simmer 5 minutes or until vegetables are tender. Drain and set aside. Cook bacon in a large skillet until crisp; remove bacon, reserve drippings in skillet. Sauté onion in drippings until wilting. Add a small amount of oil, if needed. Cut the apple into wedges. Add apple, vinegar, sugar and salt to skillet and stir. Cover and cook until apple is tender, about 3 to 4 minutes. Stir in green bean mixture and cook until well heated. Pour into a serving dish, and crumble bacon over top.

Zydeco music gets its name from *les haricots*, the Creole French term for snap beans. The folk expression *les haricots ne sont pas salles* means the beans are not salted, a saying referring to hard times when people couldn't afford salt pork to flavor their beans.

Green Beans with Almonds

2 pounds fresh or frozen green beans, trimmed
1/4 cup butter
1/2 cup chopped vegetable seasoning blend
1 clove garlic, minced
2 tablespoons fresh thyme, chopped
1/3 cup slivered almonds, toasted

Wash and cook green beans in large pot of boiling salted water until just tender (about 5 minutes). Drain beans and place in large mixing bowl with ice water to cool. Cool completely and drain. Melt butter in large skillet and sauté vegetables, garlic and half of the fresh thyme. When vegetables are limp, add beans and toss until heated through. Transfer to serving bowl and sprinkle with toasted almonds and the rest of the thyme. Serves 8 to 10.

> ➤ *Make this dish ahead by preparing green beans and storing in the refrigerator. On the day you plan to serve, sauté vegetables and thyme and prepare as directed.*

Bill's Spicy Baked Beans

1/2 cup Masterpiece mesquite barbeque sauce
1/4 cup jalapeno mustard
1 large can of pork and beans (about 28 ounces)

Preheat oven to 350 degrees F. Mix well and bake about forty minutes or until bubbling and beginning to brown on the edges. Makes 6 servings.

Crabmeat and Shrimp-Stuffed Mirliton
From <u>The Encyclopedia of Cajun & Creole Cuisine</u>
Chef John Folse, CEC, AAC, Owner & CEO
Chef John Folse & Company, Gonzales; www.jfolse.com

6 mirlitons, sliced lengthwise
1 pound jumbo lump crabmeat
1 pound (70 to 90 count) shrimp, peeled and
      deveined
1/4 pound butter
1 cup diced onions
1 cup diced celery
1/2 cup diced red bell peppers
1/4 cup minced garlic
1 tablespoon chopped basil
Salt and black pepper to taste
Granulated garlic to taste
Louisiana hot sauce to taste
1/4 cup chopped parsley
2 cups seasoned Italian bread crumbs, divided
12 pats butter

Preheat oven to 375 degrees F. Boil sliced mirlitons in lightly salted water 30 to 40 minutes or until meat is tender enough to scoop from shells. Once tender, remove from water and cool. Using a teaspoon, remove seeds and gently scoop all meat out of shell, being careful not to tear shell. Discard excess liquid accumulated while scooping meat. Reserve meat and save shells for stuffing. In a 12-inch, cast iron skillet, melt 1/4 pound butter over medium-high heat and sauté onions, celery, bell peppers, minced garlic and basil for 3 to 5 minutes or until vegetables are wilted. Blend in shrimp and cook 2 to 3 minutes or until pink and curled. Mix in reserved meat from mirlitons. Cook 15 to 20 minutes, chopping

(continued)

large pieces with a cooking spoon. After most of liquid has evaporated, remove from heat and season with salt, pepper, granulated garlic, hot sauce and parsley. Fold in crabmeat, being careful not to break lumps. Sprinkle in approximately 1 1/2 cups breadcrumbs to absorb any excess liquid and to hold stuffing intact. Divide mixture into 12 equal portions and stuff into hollowed-out shells. Place stuffed mirlitons on baking pan and sprinkle with remaining bread crumbs. Top each mirliton with 1 pat of butter. Bake 30 minutes or until golden brown. Serve one mirliton half as a vegetable or two halves as an entrée. Makes 6 Servings.

Mirliton, which originated in Mexico, is known by many Americans as chayote squash or vegetable pear and by the French as christophene. The vegetable was brought to Bayou Country by the Canary Islanders, or Los Isleños, who relocated to Louisiana when Spain took ownership of the territory from France. This South Louisiana delicacy is wonderful when stuffed with shrimp and crabmeat.—Chef John Folse

Butterbeans with Shrimp

1 pound dried butterbeans or 2 pounds fresh
3 tablespoons oil
3 tablespoons flour
1 medium onion, chopped
1 pound shrimp
Salt and cayenne pepper

Cook beans in just enough water to cover. When beans are about 1/2 hour from being cooked, make a white roux with the oil and flour. Add chopped onion to the roux; cook until the onions are soft. Add shrimp and sauté until a nice pink. Add cooked beans with water and let simmer until a rich gravy is formed. Add salt and red pepper to taste. To thicken gravy, mash some of the beans with spoon. Makes 8 to10 servings.

Honey Ginger Carrots

3 tablespoons honey
3 tablespoons butter
1/2 teaspoon salt
1 package carrots, sliced
1/4 teaspoon ground ginger
1/4 teaspoon cinnamon

Combine all ingredients in a saucepan. Cover and cook over medium heat. Stir occasionally. Cook 20 minutes or until the carrots are tender. 4 servings.

Sweet Potato Casserole

2 cans of sweet potatoes, drained
1/2 to 1 cup of sugar
1/2 teaspoon salt
2 eggs, beaten
1/2 stick of margarine
1/4 cup milk
1/2 teaspoon vanilla

Preheat oven to 350 degrees F. Spray casserole dish with Pam. Mash the potatoes and combine with the remaining casserole ingredients. Put in the casserole dish.

Topping

1 cup of brown sugar, packed
1/3 cup flour
1/3 stick of butter or margarine, melted
1 cup pecans, chopped (optional)

Mix the topping ingredients with a fork and crumble over the top of the potatoes. Bake for 40 minutes or until hot.

Sweet potatoes, or Louisiana yams, cannot be successfully baked immediately after being harvested. They must be cured for at least 10 days while the starch turns to sugar. Many commercial yams are kiln-dried to speed up the process. The orange-skinned Louisiana yam is sweeter, moister and softer than those grown in other states.

Honey and Rosemary Roasted Red Potatoes

Executive Chef Scott McCue, Mr. Lester's Cypress Bayou Casino, Charenton

4 pounds red potatoes (same as used for a
    crawfish boil)
4 cups vegetable oil
1/2 cup honey
1 tablespoon chopped fresh rosemary
1 1/2 tablespoons chopped fresh garlic
1 tablespoon Cajun seasoning

Place oil in a sauce pan with deep sides, and place over medium high heat. Cut potatoes into 1/2 inch cubes and rinse under cold water. Drain well, and pat dry. Fry potatoes until golden brown. While the potatoes are frying, heat the honey over a medium heat just until it loosens up and thins out. Add the fresh rosemary and garlic. When potatoes are done, drain well and place into a serving bowl. Toss with the honey, rosemary and garlic mixture, and season with the Cajun seasoning. Makes 10 to 12 servings.

> ➤ *This is a very simple and tasty side dish that will also hold well if being served at family get-togethers where the food is laid out on a table for a period of time. – Scott McCue*

Rosemary, the lasting symbol of remembrance, loyalty and friendship, is especially valued at Christmas for its ornamental and culinary uses. Small upright rosemary bushes are trained as topiaries for tabletop decorations, and fragrant wreaths and garlands of rosemary welcome visitors to holiday festivities. –Sarah Liberta

Shrimp and Eggplant Casserole

1/4 cup butter
3 ribs celery, chopped
1 large onion, chopped
1 bell pepper, chopped
3 cloves garlic, chopped
3 medium eggplant, peeled and chopped in
     cubes
1/2 cup chicken broth
1 1/2 pounds shrimp, cleaned and cut into
     pieces
2 eggs, beaten well
1 cup crushed crackers or breadcrumbs
1 cup Parmesan cheese
Salt, pepper and Cajun seasoning

Preheat oven to 350 degrees F. Sauté the celery, onion, garlic and bell pepper in butter until tender. Season eggplant with salt, pepper and Cajun seasoning. Add chopped eggplant and chicken broth to vegetables and simmer 10 to 20 minutes. Add shrimp and cook until they begin turning pink. Adjust seasoning to taste. Mix in egg and crackers or breadcrumbs. Pour mixture into casserole dish. Top with more crumbs and Parmesan cheese. Bake about 20 to 25 minutes or until eggplant is tender.

Broccoli Casserole

1 large onion, chopped
1/2 stick butter
3 packages frozen, chopped broccoli, thawed
1 can sliced mushrooms
1/2 cup chopped, blanched almonds
1/2 cup bread crumbs
2 cans cream of mushroom soup
8 ounces Mexican Velveeta cheese

Preheat oven to 350 degrees F. In large pan, sauté onion in butter. Add broccoli and cook until tender. Add mushroom soup, cheese, mushrooms and half of the almonds. Pour into medium-size casserole dish and top with the remaining almonds and breadcrumbs. Bake until bubbly. Serves 9 or 10.

> ➢ *If you're cooking for a crowd, you can add cooked rice to make the dish go farther. It's a delicious and rich vegetable casserole.*

Rice Dressing

1 to 2 tablespoons vegetable oil
2 pounds of lean ground beef
1 large onion, chopped
1 large bell pepper, chopped
      1/4 teaspoon minced garlic
3 stalks celery, chopped
1 (16-ounce) package Richard's frozen dressing
      mix, thawed
1 (16-ounce) package Savoy's frozen dressing mix,
      thawed
6 cups cooked rice
1 bunch green onions, chopped
1 bunch chopped parsley
Salt, red and black pepper

In large heavy pot, brown the ground meat, breaking into small pieces. When beginning to brown well, add chopped onion, bell pepper, garlic and celery. Cook until vegetables wilt. Add dressing mixes to the pot, stirring well. Cover the pot and cook on low heat, checking to add water as needed. Season with salt, black and red pepper. Allow to simmer to blend flavors. Spoon rice into mixture, blending well. Add chopped green onions and parsley; mix in. Serves 12.

Oyster, rice or cornbread dressing—which one is best? All three are used in Louisiana, with cornbread dressing more popular in North Louisiana and rice dressing, with or without oysters, and oyster dressing with French bread more popular in the southern part of the state.

Dried Cranberry and Wild Pecan
Rice Dressing
Conrad Rice Mill, New Iberia; www.conradricemill.com

1 (14 1/2-ounce) can chicken broth
1 (7-ounce) box Konriko Wild Pecan rice
1/4 cup butter or margarine
4 ounces uncooked chicken livers, chopped
2 cups chopped onion
1 1/2 cups chopped celery
1 tart apple, peeled and diced
1 tablespoon fresh thyme leaves
1 teaspoon chopped fresh sage
1/2 teaspoon salt
1/4 teaspoon ground red pepper
3/4 cup coarsely broken toasted pecans
3/4 cup sweetened dried cranberries
1/3 cup chopped parsley

Bring chicken broth to a boil in a medium saucepan;
add rice and return to a boil. Cover, reduce heat to a
simmer, and cook 20 to 25 minutes or until rice is
tender and broth is absorbed. Melt butter in a large
skillet over medium heat. Add liver and cook 1 minute,
stirring often. Add diced onion, celery, apple, thyme,
sage, salt and red pepper; cook 5 minutes or until
vegetables are tender, stirring often. Stir in pecans,
cranberries, parsley and warm rice. Mix well. Serves 8.

> Konriko was trademarked in 1950 as an acronym for
> Conrad Rice Company. The Conrad Rice Mill in New
> Iberia is listed on the National Register of Historic
> Places. It's one of the oldest rice mills in America. Tour
> the mill, and visit the store for unique souvenirs and a
> variety of Konriko products.

Oyster Dressing

1 loaf day-old French bread, sliced and lightly
    toasted
1 1/2 sticks butter
3 cloves garlic, minced
2/3 cup celery, chopped
1 bell pepper, chopped
2/3 cup onion, chopped
2 bunches green onions, finely chopped
1/3 cup minced parsley
3 teaspoons poultry seasoning
3 teaspoons salt
1/8 teaspoon pepper
1 pint oysters in liquid, or more
2 1/2 cups turkey or chicken stock
2 hard-boiled eggs (optional)

Preheat oven to 350 degrees F. Toast bread until firm
enough to cut into cubes. Cut bread into small cubes,
and set aside. Melt butter in large saucepan. Add celery,
green onions, green pepper, garlic and onion and cook
until onion is golden. Stir in bread cubes. Add parsley
and seasonings. Mix well. Drain liquor from oysters into
a small pan. Heat to boiling point. Add oysters and
simmer until oysters begin to curl. Add oysters, oyster
liquid, turkey stock and cut-up eggs to stuffing mix. Mix
well. Put in 9 x 13 inch baking dish. Cover and bake
until hot. Serves about 12 people.

Oyster dressing is a Gulf Coast tradition, particularly
popular in New Orleans. Start with a good loaf of
French bread in a paper wrapper and let it sit a day or
two to get stale. If you are short on time, use seasoned
stuffing mix.

Bonanno's Italian Sausage Rice Dressing
Gary Bonanno's Catering and Strike Zone Charters
Baton Rouge, www.batonrougecaterer.net

1 pound of ground meat
1 pound mild or spicy Italian sausage, casing
    removed
1 large yellow onion, chopped
1 tablespoon garlic, minced
1 tablespoon fennel seeds
Salt and black pepper to taste
1 teaspoon of cayenne pepper
3 cups of cooked parboiled rice
1 can of cream of mushroom soup
1 (15-ounce) can low sodium chicken stock
1 large can of sliced mushrooms, drained
3 stalks of celery, chopped

Preheat oven to 325 degrees F. Brown the meat and sausage in large skillet over medium high heat. When meat is fully cooked, add onion and garlic. Season with fennel seed, salt, black pepper and cayenne pepper. Remove from heat. In a very large mixing bowl, add meat mixture, cooked rice, cream of mushroom soup, stock, mushrooms and chopped celery. Combine well. Place dressing in a large greased baking dish, cover with foil and place in the oven for 1 hour. Serves 12 to 15.

> ➤ *Gary Bonanno has been in the restaurant business for over 30 years. He franchised the Cajun Café concepts, produced his own spice and product line and established deep sea charter services in Guatemala and Venice, Louisiana. He has appeared on several local and national fishing and cooking shows on ESPN.*

Cornbread Dressing

1 to 2 cups cooked chopped chicken (optional)
12 cups crumbled white, unsweetened cornbread
1 stick butter
2 cups Vidalia or Spanish onions, chopped
1 bunch celery, chopped (including leaves)
4 garlic cloves, minced
5 eggs, slightly beaten
7 1/2 cups chicken broth
1/3 cup fresh sage chopped (optional)
Salt and pepper to taste

Put the cornbread in a large mixing bowl. Melt the butter in skillet and sauté the seasonings and vegetables until soft. Add the vegetable mixture to the crumbled cornbread. Next add the beaten eggs to the mixture, and mix thoroughly. Then add 7 cups of the broth. Mix again thoroughly and let it rest for at least 10 minutes so that the broth can soak into the mixture. Add more broth, if needed. Put mixture into a greased 9 x 13 inch pan. Cover with foil. Bake in a preheated oven at 400 degrees F for 45 minutes. Remove the foil and continue baking until the dressing is golden brown, usually around another 10 to 15 minutes.

> ➤ *Boxed mixes are fine as long as they do not contain sugar or yellow corn meal. Mom used to boil the fryer a day or two ahead of time in a Dutch oven with carrots, celery, onions, parsnips and garlic. She also made her cornbread a day or two ahead of time. This didn't always work because if Dad found it, he ate it, and she would have to make it again. –Judy Turner, Baton Rouge*

Wild Mushroom Bread Pudding
Chef Yvette Marie Bonanno

4 ounces olive oil
2 tablespoons butter
1 small yellow onion, minced
1 tablespoon garlic, minced
1 1/2 quarts mushrooms, rough chopped –
    white domestic, Portobello, morels,
    shiitake, chanterelles, oyster mushrooms
Salt and fresh ground pepper, to taste
2 ounces white wine
2 tablespoons Italian flat-leaf parsley, minced
1 tablespoon fresh thyme, chopped
6 whole large eggs
3 cups heavy cream
3 cups whole milk
1 wheel Boursin cheese
1 gallon diced French bread, croissants or stale
    white bread

Preheat the oven to 325 degrees F. In a large hot sauté pan add oil, onion, butter, garlic and mushrooms. Allow to sauté, and season with salt and pepper. Deglaze with white wine and reduce moisture. Remove from heat. Add herbs, and allow to cool. In a large mixing bowl, combine eggs, cream, milk, Boursin cheese, bread and mushrooms. Place mixture in a 9 x 13 inch greased casserole dish and bake for one hour or until set.

> ➢ *To deglaze, add the wine, which will quickly boil. Loosen up the bits left in the skillet while stirring.*

Stuffed Artichokes

4 medium artichokes
1 cup cooked rice
1 1/2 cups Italian bread crumbs
1 egg
1 large onion, chopped fine
1/2 cup grated Romano or Parmesan cheese
1 tablespoon parsley, chopped fine
1 teaspoon granulated garlic
1 teaspoon salt
1/2 teaspoon pepper
1-2 tablespoons Italian dressing or olive oil to
    moisten

Wash and trim artichokes, cutting off tips of leaves and leveling bottom stems so artichokes sit upright. Mix rice, bread crumbs, egg, onion, cheese, parsley and seasonings. Moisten mixture with Italian dressing or olive oil. Pull back leaves of artichoke to add stuffing, working from the bottom layer up. Pack artichokes in bottom of large pot, placing close together. Add 1/2 to 1 inch of water in bottom. Drizzle tops with Italian dressing or olive oil. Bring water to a boil. Cover pot and reduce to simmer. Cook for 50 to 70 minutes—until leaves come off easily.

> ➤ *This traditional Italian dish is a popular side for holiday meals. To use as a main course, add chopped meat or seafood and serve with a salad and hot bread.*

Nonie's Cabbage Casserole

1 large head of cabbage
2 tablespoons butter
1 medium onion, chopped
1/2 pound Velveeta cheese, chopped
1 can cream of mushroom soup
1 to 2 cups Italian bread crumbs

Preheat oven to 350 degrees F. Chop cabbage. Place in medium pan with salted water to cover. Boil until tender. Drain. Sauté onion in butter until clear. Add cheese and melt. Add crumbs and cabbage and mix together. Put mixture in lightly greased medium-size casserole dish and bake for 30 minutes.

Lucky Hoppin' John

1 pound smoked sausage, sliced
2 tablespoons olive oil
1 1/2 cups chopped vegetable seasoning blend
3 (15-ounce) cans jalapeno flavored black-
        eyed peas, rinsed and drained
4 cups cooked rice
1/2 teaspoon Cajun seasoning or to taste

Brown sausage in olive oil in stock pot. Add vegetables and cook until transparent. Stir in black-eyed peas and seasoning and simmer for 20 minutes. Add cooked rice and stir together.

On New Year's Day cabbage is traditionally eaten to bring financial health in the New Year, along with black-eyed peas and pork for good luck. Bonne Chance!

Hanley-Gueno Neapolitan Presepio; Lafayette, Louisiana

Les Entrées

Cornish Hens with Herb Butter
Chef Marcelle Bienvenu, Instructor
John Folse Culinary Institute, Nicholls State University

6 Rock Cornish hens (3/4 to 1 pound each)
1/2 teaspoon cayenne
1 teaspoon salt, more or less to taste
1 cup chopped parsley
1 1/2 sticks unsalted butter, softened
1/2 cup snipped fresh chives
2 tablespoons chopped fresh rosemary
3 tablespoons chopped fresh thyme
2 tablespoons chopped fresh sage
3 tablespoons olive oil
1 1/2 tablespoons crumbled dried sage

Preheat the oven to 450 degrees F. Rinse the birds under cool water and pat dry. Sprinkle each, outside and inside the cavity, with the salt and cayenne. In a food processor, combine the butter, parsley, chives, rosemary, thyme and fresh sage and pulse several times to combine. Carefully separate the skin from the breast of each bird and spread about two tablespoons of the herb butter between the skin and breast. Smooth out the skin and truss.

Rub the oil over the birds and sprinkle with more salt and cayenne if desired. Rub the dried sage evenly over each bird and place in a roasting pan. Roast for 20 minutes. Reduce the heat to 350 degrees F and continue cooking until the juices run clear when pricked with a fork or pointed knife, about 40 more minutes. Baste with the pan juices during the cooking time. Serve on a bed of fresh herbs to serve. Makes 6 servings.

➢ *Perfect for an elegant meal.*

Boudin-Stuffed Cornish Hens
Yvette Marie Bonanno, Honor Graduate
Johnson and Wales Culinary University

4 Cornish hens, rinse well, pat dry
1 package Savoie Boudin Sausage, remove casing
3 ounces butter, melted
2 tablespoons Italian flat-leaf parsley, minced
2 tablespoons green onion, minced
1 tablespoon poultry seasoning
1 can chicken broth
Olive oil

Spice Blend

2 tablespoons kosher salt
1 tablespoon granulated garlic
2 tablespoons Tony Chachere's seasoning

Preheat the oven to 425 degrees F. Season the hens
inside and out with the spice blend. In a mixing bowl,
combine the boudin, butter and herbs. Fill the hen
cavity with boudin stuffing and place in a baking dish,
breast side up. Drizzle with olive oil and add chicken
broth to the dish. Bake for 15 minutes, and then reduce
the temperature to 350 degrees F for 40 to 45 minutes,
until the internal temperature reaches 160 degrees F.
Remove from the oven and allow to rest. Serve with pan
drippings. Serves 4.

> ➤ *Yvette owned three businesses in Baton Rouge:*
> *Bonanno's Fine Catering, Yvette Marie's Café, and*
> *Taste by Yvette Bonanno in Baton Rouge. She sold her*
> *businesses in 2008 and moved to Denver with her*
> *husband. She is currently providing private chef services*
> *for several families.*

Seafood Stuffed Turkey Breast with Tomato Cream Sauce

Chef Roman Landry, Mr. Lester's
Cypress Bayou Casino, Charenton

2 uncooked turkey breasts boneless, skinless
3 tablespoons Creole seasoning
4 tablespoons butter
1 cup diced onions
1/2 cup diced red bell pepper
3 tablespoons chopped garlic
2 pounds sliced mushrooms, such as shiitake or
    portabella
1 pound Louisiana crawfish tails
1 pound small gumbo shrimp, peeled
1/2 cup white wine
1 cup grated pepper jack cheese
1/2 cup plain breadcrumbs
2 tablespoons fresh chopped parsley
2 tablespoons fresh chopped green onions
Butcher twine
Salt, ground black pepper to taste

Preheat the oven to 325 degrees F. Place the breast onto cutting board. Butterfly by making a series of small cuts vertically in the meat, without cutting all the way through. Place a sheet of plastic wrap over the turkey meat. Pound it with a mallet until 1/2 inch thin and flat. Remove the plastic wrap and sprinkle the meat with 1 tablespoon Creole seasoning. Heat the butter in a large skillet over medium high heat. Sauté the onions, peppers and mushrooms for 3 minutes. Add garlic and seafood, and cook for another 5 minutes. Then add wine, and cook until wine has evaporated, about 5 minutes. Remove from heat and allow the stuffing to cool. Add

(continued)

the cheese, breadcrumbs, parsley, green onions, to the stuffing mixture, and mix well. Spread stuffing over the turkey; roll up like a pinwheel, tucking in the ends. Lay 4 pieces of twine under the roll crosswise and tie. Sprinkle the roll with the remaining 1 tablespoon of Creole seasoning. Place the roll on a baking sheet and roast until cooked, about 40 to 45 minutes, basting occasionally. Remove from oven and allow to rest. Cut into 12 to 14 slices. Serve with roasted garlic sun-dried tomato cream sauce.

Roasted Garlic Sun-Dried Tomato Cream Sauce

> 1 tablespoon butter
> 1 tablespoon diced onions
> 3 tablespoons roasted garlic
> 1 cup chopped sun-dried tomatoes
> 1/2 quart heavy cream
> 1 (16-ounce) can chicken broth
> 1/4 cup fresh chopped green onion
> 1/4 cup fresh chopped parsley
> Salt and freshly ground black pepper, to taste
> 2 tablespoons blond roux (butter and flour)

Melt butter in a saucepan. Add onions, garlic and tomatoes. Cook on medium heat for 5 minutes, and then add the heavy cream, chicken stock, green onions and parsley. Bring sauce to a boil, and then add roux. (To make a roux: Use equal parts butter and flour. Melt butter gently, add flour. Stir and cook over medium heat. The longer you cook the roux, the darker the color. Generally it takes about four minutes to make a blond roux.) Stir in well, and let simmer for 10 minutes. Add salt and pepper to taste. Serve hot over cooked, stuffed turkey roll. Makes 12 to 14 servings.

Pot Roasted Duck

6 large ducks
1 large onion, chopped
4 stalks celery chopped
1 large bell pepper, chopped
1 cup red wine vinegar
2 tablespoons Worcestershire sauce
4 slices of bacon
6 pods of garlic
2 cans mushrooms
Steak sauce
3 cups vegetable oil
Red and black pepper, salt, garlic powder

Preheat oven to 375 degrees F. Mix onion, celery, bell pepper, red wine vinegar, red and black pepper, salt, garlic powder and Worcestershire to make stuffing. Make a pocket in the breast of the duck. Place a heaping tablespoon of the stuffing mixture into each breast. Slice each piece of bacon into three. Put a garlic half into each pocket; then seal pocket with a piece of bacon. Season outside of duck and inside cavity with salt, peppers, garlic powder, Worcestershire and wine vinegar. Cover duck and marinate in refrigerator several hours. Spray large pot or roaster with Pam and add 3 cups vegetable oil to pot. Place ducks in pot and cover. Cook 3 1/2 to 4 hours or until tender. Uncover pot to brown ducks. Take ducks out of pot; drain oil, but leave drippings. Add onion, bell pepper and celery and saute until tender. Add 2 cans mushrooms, steak sauce and 3 to 4 cups of water to make gravy. Season to taste.

➤ *This recipe is from Jeanne Saal of Gueydan, home of the Duck Festival.*

Rabbit Pie

1 rabbit, cut into pieces
3 tablespoons butter
2 tablespoons each of chopped onion, parsley.
1/4 cup flour
Refrigerated ready-made pie crust

Preheat oven to 350 degrees F. Cover the rabbit pieces with salted water and simmer until tender. Remove meat from the pot and save the broth. Carefully remove bones from rabbit meat. Heat 3 tablespoons of butter in a skillet. Add chopped onion and parsley. Add salt to taste. Cook vegetables until wilting in the skillet; gradually add 3 tablespoons of flour and stir until the flour is absorbed. Add 1 cup of broth from rabbit, stirring until smooth. Simmer about 4 minutes until mixture thickens. If mixture needs to thicken further, whisk in another tablespoon of flour. Fill deep dish with mixture and cover with pie crust. Bake until brown.

Christmas tree farms help the environment by providing a habitat for birds and wildlife, removing dust and pollen from the air and helping boost oxygen levels. About 59 percent of Christmas trees nationwide are later recycled in statewide and community programs.

Chicken Pinwheels
Patti Constantin, Designs in Catering, New Orleans
American Heart Association Culinary Hearts Cook Off winner

8 boneless, skinless chicken breasts
2 tablespoons chopped garlic
4 tablespoons chopped eschallots or yellow
    onions
Small amount olive oil
2 ounces Neufchatel cheese, softened
1 1/2 cups cooked spinach, liquid squeezed out
4 ounces Feta cheese
Red and black pepper to taste
4 cups cooked brown rice

Preheat oven to 350 degrees F. Sauté garlic and eschallots in olive oil. Mix with Neufchatel cheese until smooth. Chop spinach finely and add with feta cheese into cheese mixture. Season with pepper. Chill. Butterfly chicken breast. Place portion of spinach on each breast; roll in jellyroll style. Dust rolls with flour and sauté lightly (seam side down) in olive oil. Cook until brown and seam is sealed. Chill. When ready to serve, slice rolls into four pinwheels. Cook under broiler until done. Serve over brown rice and top with wine sauce and pears.

Madeira Wine Sauce

2 quarts chicken stock
1 large onion, chopped
2 tablespoons French eschallots, cut coarsely
1 tablespoon garlic, minced
28 ounces Madeira wine
1 teaspoon marjoram
2 pears

(continued)
Cook all ingredients except pears until reduced by half. Puree to thicken. Drizzle sauce over pinwheels before serving. Julienne pears to garnish. Serves 8. Sauce recipe can be cut in half.

Red Beans and Rice

> 1 pound dried red beans (Camellia brand)
> 1 bell pepper, chopped
> 2 onions, chopped
> 2 cloves garlic, minced
> 1 rib celery, chopped
> 1 pound smoked sausage, sliced
> 1 pound ham, cut in pieces
> 1 bay leaf
> Salt, pepper and cayenne to taste

Wash beans and remove any bad beans or particles. Cover beans with water, and soak overnight to speed up cooking time. When ready to cook, drain water from beans. Place in a large pot with water to cover, and bring to a boil. Sauté cut up vegetables, sausage and ham in a little oil until sausage is browned and vegetables are clear. Add to beans and water with bay leaf and seasonings. Simmer for 1 to 2 hours until beans are soft. To thicken mixture, mash some of the beans against side of pan. Serve over rice.

> ➤ *This New Orleans recipe is from Charles Currie.*

Red beans and rice is a New Orleans favorite traditionally served on Monday, which was wash day. Add French bread and a salad, and you have a complete meal for a crowd.

Oven Barbecued Brisket

4 to 5-pound boneless beef brisket, trimmed
Salt and pepper
Granulated garlic
1 cup barbeque sauce
1 cup water

Preheat oven to 275 degrees F. Liberally rub both sides
of brisket with salt, pepper and garlic. Cook in 9 x 13
inch pan covered tightly with foil with no water added,
allowing one hour per pound. Before the last hour of
cooking, remove brisket and slice on the diagonal
(against the grain). Return to pan and add barbecue
sauce mixed with water. Cook one hour longer,
uncovered. Serves 8 to 10.

Barbecue Sauce

14 ounce bottle catsup (1 cup)
1/2 cup Worcestershire sauce
1/2 cup vinegar
1/2 cup brown sugar
2 tablespoons yellow mustard
2 tablespoons Tabasco
1 can beer
1 tablespoon butter
Juice of one lemon
Salt

Stir all ingredients together in medium pot and simmer
uncovered until sauce is thick—approximately one hour.
Makes 1 quart.

Crawfish Stuffed Tenderloin

Beef tenderloin, trimmed
Chopped fresh rosemary, Dijon mustard, honey
1/2 pound cleaned crawfish tails
Cracked black pepper and salt, to taste
Cooking twine

Preheat oven to 500 degrees F. Split loin down the middle. Line inside of loin lightly with crushed rosemary. Season crawfish with salt and pepper and place in middle of loin. Fold over meat; tie firmly with twine to keep the stuffing enclosed. Season outside with cracked pepper. Mix rosemary, honey and mustard; rub onto meat. Roast in oven for 20 to 30 minutes, depending on the size of loin and desired doneness. Let the loin rest 10 to 15 minutes before slicing and serving.

Cream Sauce with Crawfish (Optional)

2 tablespoons butter
2 tablespoons flour
1/2 cup milk, heated
1/2 to 1 cup heavy cream
Dash of nutmeg, salt and pepper to taste
1/2 pound crawfish tails

Melt butter over medium heat. Add flour; stir until blended. Gradually add milk, stirring until sauce begins to boil and thicken. Reduce heat; simmer 5 minutes, stirring frequently. Stir in cream. Season with salt, pepper, and dash of nutmeg. Add crawfish and heat.

> ➤ *Linda Griffis Smart, Lafayette, created this recipe after tasting a similar tenderloin about 25 years ago. She has served this dish every Christmas since.*

Grillades
Chef Marcelle Bienvenu, Food Columnist

4 pounds boneless beef or veal round steak
      (about 1/4 inch thick)
1 tablespoon salt
1 teaspoon cayenne
1/2 teaspoon black pepper
1/2 teaspoon garlic powder
1/2 cup flour
1/2 cup vegetable oil
3 medium yellow onions, chopped
2 medium green bell peppers, chopped
3 ribs celery, chopped
3 cups whole canned tomatoes, crushed with
      juice
2 cups beef broth
1/2 cup dry red wine
1/2 teaspoon dried tarragon leaves
1/2 teaspoon dried basil leaves
2 bay leaves
1/2 cup finely chopped green onions
2 tablespoons finely chopped fresh parsley leaves

Remove fat from meat and cut into 2-inch squares.
Combine salt, cayenne, black pepper and garlic in a
small bowl. Have the flour at hand. Lay several pieces of
the meat on a cutting board and sprinkle with seasoning
mix and a little of the flour. With a meat mallet, pound
each piece of meat until slightly flattened. Flip the pieces
over and repeat the process. Do this with all the meat. In
a large, heavy pot or Dutch oven, heat the oil over
medium high heat. Add the meat, several pieces at a
time, and brown evenly on both sides. Once the meat
browns, transfer to a platter. When all meat is browned,

(continued)
return to the pot. Add yellow onions, bell peppers and celery and cook, stirring, until vegetables are soft and golden (8 to 10 minutes). Add the tomatoes and their liquid and reduce heat to medium-low. Add broth, wine, bay leaves, tarragon and basil. Stir to mix and simmer uncovered, stirring occasionally. Cook until the meat is very tender (about 1 1/2 hours). If mixture becomes dry, add a little water or more broth. Adjust seasoning if necessary with salt and pepper to taste. When ready to serve add the green onions and parsley. Serve with grits.

> ➤ *On the weekend after Thanksgiving, Marcelle and her husband make a triple batch of grillades to store in the freezer for use during the Christmas holidays. Usually on the Sunday between Christmas and New Year's, they invite friends and family for brunch with Baked Grits and Grillades, which they serve with a seasonal fruit compote and buttered biscuits.*

Baked Grits
Chef Marcelle Bienvenu, Cookbook Author

2 cups yellow grits, cooked according to package directions
3 large eggs, slightly beaten
1/2 pound grated cheddar cheese
1 cup milk
1 stick butter

Preheat oven to 350 degrees F. After the grits are cooked, add the eggs, cheese, milk and butter and stir until all is blended and the cheese and butter are completely melted. Pour into a 2-quart baking dish and bake for about 45 minutes. Makes 10 to 12 servings.

Oyster Cobbler with Andouille Crust
Yvette Bonanno, American Culinary Foundation
Chef of the Year 2002

Crust

3 whole eggs
1 1/2 cups flour
1/2 cup Italian bread crumbs
3 tablespoons butter
1 link Andouille sausage, rough chopped

In a food processor add eggs, bread crumbs and flour. Pulse and add butter and sausage. Allow to combine, and reserve.

Filling

1 pint shucked oysters with its liquor
2 ounces olive oil
2 tablespoons butter
2 tablespoons parsley, fine chopped
2 tablespoons green onion
1 leek, white portion only
2 shallots, peeled and diced
Bay leaf
1 tablespoon garlic minced
1 can artichoke hearts, julienned
2 ounces white wine
1 can cream of mushroom soup
1 can cream of celery soup
Salt and pepper to taste

Preheat the oven to 375 degrees F. In a sauté pan add oil, butter, leeks, shallots, bay leaf, parsley, green onions

(continued)

and garlic. Add artichoke hearts and allow to sauté.
Deglaze with white wine. Season and add oyster liquor.
Add cream of mushroom and cream of celery soup and
heat through. Remove from heat and add oysters.
Assemble oyster mixture topped with Andouille crust in
ramekins. Bake for 25 to 30 minutes.

Crab au Gratin

1 medium onion, chopped
1 bell pepper, chopped
1 rib celery, chopped
1/2 cup butter
1/4 cup flour
1 1/2 cups half and half
1/2 teaspoon black pepper
2 teaspoons salt
1/2 teaspoon cayenne pepper
1 tablespoon Worcestershire sauce
1 pound crabmeat
1/2 to 1 cup grated cheddar cheese
1/2 cup breadcrumbs

Preheat oven to 350 degrees F. Sauté onion, celery and
bell pepper in butter in heavy skillet. Stir in flour until
absorbed. Add half and half gradually, constantly
stirring. Add salt, pepper and Worcestershire sauce.
Cook 5 minutes. Add crab, and pour into greased
casserole dish. Sprinkle with grated cheese and
breadcrumbs. Bake for 20 minutes. Serves 4. Recipe can
be doubled.

Shrimp and Andouille Cassoulet
Brian Landry, Chef
Louisiana Seafood Board

4 pounds fresh head-on shrimp (16 to 20 count)
2 tablespoons plus 1 teaspoon Creole seasoning
3 cups low sodium chicken broth
2 tablespoons olive oil
1 pound Andouille sausage (or smoked sausage
    or bacon)—cut into 1/4 inch pieces
1 sweet onion, diced
4 celery stalks, diced
4 garlic cloves, minced
1 teaspoon dried oregano
10 whole peeled canned Roma tomatoes (about
    28 ounces)
3 teaspoons Worcestershire sauce
4 (15-ounce) cans white kidney, cannellini
    or other white beans
2 teaspoons fresh thyme
1 bunch green onions, chopped
3 cups breadcrumbs (use panko, if possible)
1 1/2 cups ground Parmesan cheese
3 tablespoons olive oil
Salt and pepper

Peel and devein shrimp. Season with 2 tablespoons of Creole seasoning. Place the shrimp shells in 1.5 quart saucepan with the chicken broth and place over medium heat. Allow to simmer.

In a large skillet or small Dutch oven, heat olive oil over medium-high heat. Add Andouille and brown. Add onion, celery, garlic, Creole seasoning and oregano and

(continued)

cook until vegetables are tender and translucent. Crush tomatoes over skillet and add Worcestershire. Rinse beans under cold water and add to skillet. Add thyme and green onions. Strain shells from broth and add broth to skillet. Allow beans and sausage to simmer for 15 to 20 minutes. While beans are simmering, mix breadcrumbs, Parmesan, olive oil, salt and pepper. Add shrimp and allow to cook for 8 to 10 minutes. Cover skillet with breadcrumb mixture, and place under broiler for 2 to 3 minutes until breadcrumbs are brown. Serves 8.

Optional Garnish

Reserve 8 shrimp and peel only the body, leaving the head and tail intact. Season with Creole seasoning. Heat 2 tablespoons of olive oil in medium skillet. Cook shrimp for about 2 minutes on each side until they are browned and cooked through. Arrange shrimp on top of cassoulet once it has been browned under the broiler.

> ➢ *While it can be served year round, I think it is a great recipe for dinners in the colder months.–Chef Brian Landry*

Louisiana celebrates the shrimp industry with two major festivals: the Shrimp and Petroleum Festival in Morgan City and the Shrimp Festival in Delcambre. The Louisiana Shrimp and Petroleum Festival is the state's largest and oldest chartered harvest festival, and Delcambre is home to one of the area's most productive shrimp fleets. Both festivals feature boat parades and blessing of the fleet.

Shrimp Creole

1 tablespoon vegetable oil
1/4 cup bell pepper, chopped
1/4 cup onions, chopped
1 tablespoon Tabasco sauce
1/2 cup chopped tomatoes
1/4 cup fresh mushrooms, chopped
1/4 cup lemon juice
1 pound peeled shrimp, no heads
2 to 3 cups cooked rice

In a heavy pot, add vegetable oil. Begin heating on low, and add bell pepper and onions. When they begin to wilt, add chopped tomatoes, lemon juice, Tabasco sauce and mushrooms. Mix and simmer a few minutes on low heat. Add shrimp to mixture, making certain that shell pieces have all been removed. Cover pot and simmer on low, stirring occasionally. Shrimp cook quickly; they should be pinkish instead of white to be ready. Serve over portions of cooked rice. Serves 4.

SCALLION

Louisiana shrimpers catch 90 to 120 million pounds of brown and white shrimp each year. White shrimp season is April through December, and brown shrimp season is April through February.

Crawfish Cornbread
Ollie Bryan and Louis Cascio, Crawdaddy's Kitchen
Shreveport; www.crawdaddyskitchen.com

1/2 cup liquid butter (or melted butter)
2 cups bell pepper, chopped
2 cups onions, chopped
1/2 teaspoon garlic powder
1/2 pound crawfish tails
2 boxes (8-ounce) Jiffy cornbread mix
2 eggs
1/2 cup milk
2 cans Rotel tomatoes, drained

Preheat oven to 350 degrees F. Saute onions and bell pepper in liquid butter until tender. Sprinkle on garlic powder and mix well with vegetables. Add crawfish tails and cook until half done. Combine cornbread mix, milk and eggs in a separate bowl and blend until smooth. Add tomatoes and stir until mixed, stir in crawfish tail mixture; mix well. Pour into a well-greased 9 x 13 inch aluminum pan. Bake at 350 degrees F for 45 to 60 minutes until golden brown. Brush top with butter. Cool before cutting.

> ➤ *Customers rave about crawfish cornbread at Crawdaddy's Kitchen. The spicy sweet flavor is scrumptious.*

Meat Pie
Official Natchitoches Meat Pie Festival™

Filling
1 teaspoon shortening
1 pound ground meat
1 pound ground pork meat
1 bunch green onions, chopped
1 pod garlic, minced
1 bell pepper, chopped
1 medium onion chopped
Salt, black pepper and red pepper to taste
1 tablespoon flour

Melt shortening in heavy pot. Add meat and seasonings. When meat is completely done but not dry, remove from heat and drain excess liquid. Stir in 1 tablespoon flour. Let this mixture cool completely before assembling meat pies.

Crust
1 quart plain flour
2 teaspoons salt
1 teaspoon baking powder
1 cup shortening
2 eggs
1 cup milk

Sift dry ingredients together. Cut in shortening. Beat egg and add to milk. Work gradually into dry ingredients until proper consistency to roll. Break into small pieces and roll very thin and cut into rounds using a saucer as a guide.

(continued)
To Assemble:
Place a large tablespoon of cooled meat along edge and halfway in the center of round dough. Fold the other half over, making edges meet and seal with water. Form edges with fork. Drop in deep fat and cook until golden brown. Drain and serve hot. Makes approximately 18.

> ➢ *This recipe courtesy of Mrs. L.J. Melder, Natchitoches*

Pulled Pork

Boneless trimmed pork roast, 3 to 4 pounds
1 can condensed French Onion Soup
1 cup of robust barbeque sauce
1/4 cup cider vinegar
3 tablespoons of packed brown sugar

Cut the roast into two or three pieces, and put in crockpot. In a medium bowl, combine the soup, barbeque sauce, vinegar, and brown sugar. Mix until blended and pour over pork. Cook on low for 8 hours. After 8 hours, shred the pork and return to the crockpot. Shred pork at least 1/2 hour prior to serving. Serve on buns.

> ➢ *Cooking in the crockpot is a great solution for dinner after an activity-filled day.*

The annual Natchidoches Meat Pie Festival is held in September in the National Landmark Historic District. The festival celebrates the tasty meat pie, which has been a community favorite since it was invented in the 1700s.

Game Day Pistolettes

1 stick butter, divided
3 tablespoons and 5 tablespoons flour
1 onion, chopped
1 bell pepper, chopped
2 ribs celery, chopped
1 clove garlic, minced
      (or use 2 1/2 cups chopped vegetable
      seasoning blend instead of vegetables and
      garlic)
1 (8-ounce) pack sliced fresh mushrooms
      or 1 can (optional)
2 pounds of peeled crawfish or shrimp
18 to 20 pistolettes (oval-shaped brown and serve
      rolls)

Preheat oven to 400 degrees F. In small sauté pan, melt 3 tablespoons butter, add 3 tablespoons flour and stir constantly until blended to make a blond roux. Do not brown. Set aside. In large pot, melt remaining butter and sauté mushrooms and vegetables until vegetables are limp. Add seafood and simmer for 15 minutes. Heat roux and then slowly add to seafood mixture. Simmer for another 5 minutes to thicken. Slice pistolettes in half and scoop out some of the bread from both sides to make room for stuffing. Stuff each pistolette with heaping spoons of seafood mixture. Place in 9 x 13 inch pan. Brush tops with melted butter. Bake for about 8 minutes or until brown. These can be refrigerated or frozen until time to heat and serve.

Baked Fish
Louisiana Sisters, www.louisianasisters.net

1 pound fresh fish cut into 2 inch pieces
Salt and pepper to taste
1 jar of Louisiana Sisters Spiced Tapenade (this is
        the best part!)
1 tablespoon chopped red onion
3 tablespoons of extra virgin olive oil

Preheat oven to 400 degrees F. Grease baking dish with
olive oil. Arrange fish in pan; salt and pepper. Combine
tapenade, red onion, basil and olive oil in bowl then
spoon over fish. Bake for 20 minutes or until fish flakes
when tested with fork. This dish is delicious with angel
hair pasta and a green salad.

Easy Breaded Speckled Trout

2 to 4 filets of speckled trout
Salt and pepper to taste
Louisiana Hot Sauce
Yellow mustard
Progresso Italian Bread Crumbs
4 tablespoons butter

Dry filets, season with hot sauce, salt and pepper to taste.
Use brush to dab mustard on filets and then roll in
breadcrumbs. Heat butter in cast iron skillet. Get pan
hot, but do not burn butter. Sauté filets in butter until
done, which will not take long. Be careful not to
overcook, and turn filets only once.

> ➢ *A quick and easy way to cook fresh fish. Recipe from
> the late John Sylvest, New Roads.*

Audrey's Quiche

2 (9-inch) pie shells
1 cup onion, chopped
2 cups fresh mushrooms, coarsely chopped
1 package frozen chopped broccoli or spinach
2 tablespoons butter
1/2 to 1 teaspoon Cajun seasoning
1 teaspoon salt
Pepper to taste
6 eggs
16 ounces small curd cottage cheese
2 cups shredded cheddar cheese
1/4 to 1/2 cup milk

Bake pie shells according to package directions. Preheat oven to 350 degrees F. Sauté onion, mushrooms and spinach or broccoli in butter until onions are clear. Add seasonings and cool slightly. In medium mixing bowl, mix eggs with cottage cheese and 1/4 cup milk. Add 1 cup shredded cheese. Gradually add the sautéed onion mixture to the egg mixture. If mixture seems too thick, add more milk. Pour mixture evenly into two pie shells and top with remaining cheese. Bake for 25 to 35 minutes. Let sit 10 to 15 minutes before cutting. Pies can be frozen after baking.

> ➤ *This quiche recipe uses cottage cheese instead of heavy cream. Ingredients can be easily changed to suit tastes. Try adding chopped turkey, chicken or any other vegetables that you like.*

No-Fail Crawfish Étouffée

1 onion, chopped
1/4 cup sliced green onions
2 tablespoons butter
1 green bell pepper, chopped
1 can Rotel original tomatoes
Lots of chopped garlic
Cajun spices
1 can Golden Mushroom soup
1 pound crawfish tails

Melt butter in large skillet. Add onions, Rotel tomatoes, bell pepper and garlic. Season and sauté until vegetables are wilted. Empty can of soup into skillet and blend with vegetables. Fold in crawfish tails and heat for another 15 to 20 minutes, stirring occasionally. Serve over rice. May also be used as a dip or a sauce over fish.

Ham Fettuccine

8 ounces ham, cut in bite-sized pieces
1 cup heavy cream
1/4 cup butter
1 pound fettuccine
1 small bunch green onions, chopped
3/4 cup grated Parmesan cheese
Black pepper to taste, freshly ground

Cook fettuccine, following directions. Melt butter in a heavy skillet. Add onions and ham. Cook until golden. Season with lots of black pepper. Stir in cream and keep warm while the pasta is cooking. Drain the pasta and toss with the sauce. Stir in the cheese and serve at once. Makes 6 servings.

Busy-Day Lasagna

1 pound ground beef
1 to 2 teaspoons minced garlic (optional)
2 jars favorite spaghetti sauce
6 lasagna noodles
1 (15-ounce) container ricotta cheese
2 cups mozzarella cheese
1/3 cup Parmesan cheese

Preheat oven to 350 degrees F. Cook the noodles following directions on package. Brown the ground beef and garlic in a large skillet. Drain the meat on a paper towel and rinse the skillet. Put the meat and 1 jar of the sauce in the skillet and heat. Spray a lasagna pan or a 9 x 13 pan with Pam. Put a very small amount of the sauce from the second jar on the bottom the pan and spread. Put 1/2 of the noodles in the pan. Spread the ricotta cheese on the noodles. Sprinkle the parmesan cheese and 1/2 of the mozzarella cheese on the noodles and ricotta cheese. Add the meat-sauce mixture. Follow with the remainder of the noodles. Put the remainder of the jar of sauce on the noodles and top with the remainder of the mozzarella cheese. Bake about 30 minutes, or until lightly browned and bubbling. Serves 8.

The Zwolle Tamale Fiesta in October honors the town's Spanish and Indian heritage with a fun-filled festival offering tamales and other food, parades, activities and entertainment for all. Originally an Indian village and later occupied by the Spanish, the town became a whistle stop along the railroad in the 1800s, inspiring the townspeople to try to produce the best tamale in the country.

Hot Tamales

4 pounds ground meat
2 large onions, chopped finely
2 teaspoons garlic powder
4 1/2 teaspoons salt
2 teaspoons red pepper, or more
2 (2-ounce) bottles chili powder
1 1/2 heaping teaspoons oregano
1 1/2 heaping teaspoons cumin
1 (8-ounce) can tomato sauce
1 cup cornmeal
1/2 teaspoon salt
1 (8-ounce) can tomato sauce
1 teaspoon chili powder
Rice paper wrappers

In large bowl, mix first 9 ingredients together. Shape meat mixture into small rolls (about 1 inch). Mix one cup cornmeal with 1/2 teaspoon of salt. Dip rice paper in water. Roll each meat roll in small amount of cornmeal mixture and place on a piece of wet rice paper. Sprinkle with a generous pinch of cornmeal/salt mixture. Roll in paper with seams down and ends folded up. Crisscross tamales and layer in pot with rack on bottom. In bowl, mix one can tomato sauce, one teaspoon chili powder and a little salt. Add enough water so mixture will cover tamales and pour in pot. Anchor tamales down with a small plate and simmer on low heat for 1 1/2 hours. Makes about 80 tamales.

> ➤ *For the Tompkins family in Lafayette, making tamales together is a Christmas Eve tradition. This recipe was originally used for fundraising events at Catholic High School in New Iberia in the '70s.*

Bayou Pasta Jambalaya
Chef Damon Schexnayder

1/4 cup vegetable oil
1 pound of chicken breast, diced
1/2 pound smoked beef sausage, sliced
1/2 pound pork Tasso, diced
2 cups marinara sauce
2 quarts heavy cream
2 cups chicken stock
4 tablespoons Creole seasoning
1 cup white wine
2 tablespoons Worcestershire sauce
1 1/2 pounds penne pasta
4 ounces Tiger Sauce
1/2 cup fresh flat leaf parsley
1/2 cup green onions
1/4 cup Parmesan cheese, divided
1/4 cup green onions, chopped for garnish

Place an 8-quart stock pot on medium-high heat. Add
oil, chicken, sausage and Tasso. Let brown on all sides
for 6 to 8 minutes. Add marinara sauce, cream, stock,
Creole seasoning, Worcestershire sauce and wine.
Simmer on medium-high heat for 15 to 20 minutes or
until sauce reduces by 1/3. While the sauce is
simmering, cook the penne pasta following the
directions on the package. Remove the sauce from heat,
and add Tiger Sauce, parsley, 1/2 cup green onions and
1/2 of Parmesan cheese. Salt and pepper to taste. Pour
Cajun Tomato Cream over penne pasta, and garnish
with the remaining Parmesan and 1/4 cup green onions.

> ➤ *Damon, a native of Crowley, has helped feed displaced*
> *citizens and relief workers in hurricane seasons.*

Hanley-Gueno Neapolitan Presepio; Lafayette, Louisiana

Les Desserts

Bread Pudding

1 teaspoon nutmeg
2 cups milk
2 cups heavy cream
2 cups sugar
4 tablespoons of melted butter
3 eggs
2 tablespoons vanilla
1 cup of raisins
1 cup of chopped pecans (optional)
1 teaspoon cinnamon
1 loaf of stale French bread, broken, or 8 cups of
  any bread

Combine all ingredients and place in buttered 9 x 9 inch baking dish. Place on middle rack in cool oven. Bake at 350 degrees F for approximately 1 hour 15 minutes or until top is golden brown. Top with sauce.

Rum Sauce

1 stick of butter
1 1/2 cups of powdered sugar
1/2 cup of rum, bourbon or Amaretto
1 egg yolk

Stir butter and sugar over medium heat until all butter is absorbed. Blend in egg yolk, and continue stirring until the edges bubble. Remove from heat. Pour in bourbon gradually, stirring constantly. Sauce thickens as it cools.

> ➤ *Major Jamey Turner, Baton Rouge native, has cooked this Louisiana dish for his family and friends at Ft. Hood, West Point, Ft. Campbell and Ft. Leavenworth.*

Apple Pecan Cake

3 eggs
2 cups sugar
1 1/2 cups vegetable oil
3 cups all-purpose flour
1 teaspoon baking soda
1 teaspoon salt
3 cups chopped unpeeled apples
1 cup chopped pecans
2 teaspoons vanilla

Preheat oven to 350 degrees F. Grease and flour 10-inch tube pan. In large mixing bowl beat eggs. Add sugar and oil. Beat with electric mixer on high. In a separate bowl, mix flour, baking soda and salt. Add slowly to large mixing bowl. Batter will be stiff. Fold in apples, pecans and vanilla. Pour into prepared pan. Bake 1 hour and 15 minutes. Remove cake from oven and cool for 15 minutes before removing from pan. Pour topping over cake while it is still warm.

Topping

1 cup light brown sugar
1/2 cup butter
1/4 cup milk

Combine sugar, milk and butter in saucepan. Bring to a boil. Let boil 3 minutes. Pour over warm cake.

Yummy Yam Spice Cake
Sarah Liberta, HERBS by Sarah
www.herbsbysarah.com

3 cups sugar
1 cup vegetable oil
4 eggs
2 cups canned sweet potatoes, pureed
1 teaspoon baking powder
1 teaspoon cinnamon
1 teaspoon nutmeg
1 teaspoon allspice
3 1/2 cups all-purpose flour, sifted
1/2 teaspoon ground cloves
1 1/2 teaspoon salt
2 teaspoon baking soda
2/3 cup water
1 1/2 cups pecans, chopped
1 tablespoon banana liqueur (optional)

Preheat oven to 350 degrees F. In large mixing bowl, cream together sugar and oil. Add eggs, beating until light and fluffy. Add sweet potatoes; mix well. Sift together dry ingredients; add 1/3 to sugar mixture and mix well. Add half of water and liqueur; mix well. Repeat, ending with flour mixture. Fold in nuts. Pour into greased and floured 10-inch tube or bundt pan (or two 9 x 5 inch loaf pans, or several smaller loaf pans half full). Bake for one hour or until a fork inserted in the center comes out clean. (If using small pans, adjust time accordingly.) For muffins, grease muffin or mini-muffin tins (or line with baking papers) and bake approximately 20 to 25 minutes for 36 regular muffins or about 15 minutes for 72 mini-muffins. Makes 12 to 18 servings.

(continued)

> *I've been making variations on this cake for over forty years. Delicious any time of year, it's a special treat for the winter holidays. This is a large, moist, delicious cake; it rises 1/3 to 1/2 again. The secret ingredient, a fruity liqueur, adds an element of surprise and depth of flavor. –Sarah Liberta*

Caramel Chocolate Cake

1 box German Chocolate Cake Mix
3/4 cup melted butter
1 (14-ounce) bag caramels
1/2 cup evaporated milk
1 cup chopped nuts
1 (6-ounce) bag semisweet chocolate chips

Preheat oven in 350 degrees F. In large bowl, mix cake mix and butter by hand. Press 1/2 of mixture into a greased and floured 9 x 13 inch pan. Bake for 6 minutes. Melt caramels with evaporated milk in small saucepan. Remove cake from oven and sprinkle nuts and chocolate chips over top. Pour caramel mixture over chips. Drop remaining cake mixture by spoonful over top of cake mixture. Bake for 15 minutes. Cool in refrigerator before cutting into squares.

> *This delicious brownie-like recipe is from the Fellowship Baptist Church Cookbook, Dubach.*

Dark Chocolate Cake

1/2 cup sour milk or buttermilk
2 cups flour (1 cup may be whole wheat)
2 cups sugar
1 teaspoon cinnamon
2 teaspoons soda
2 sticks butter or margarine
2 tablespoons dark cocoa
1 cup water
2 eggs
1 teaspoon vanilla

Preheat oven to 350 degrees F. Make sour milk by
adding 1 tablespoon of vinegar to 1 cup of milk and
letting it sit 5 to 10 minutes. Using a spoon, mix dry
ingredients in a mixing bowl. Heat the butter, water and
cocoa until the butter is melted and all are mixed
together. Pour into the dry ingredients and add the eggs,
sour milk and vanilla and beat until well mixed. Pour
into a 9 x 13 inch pan and bake for 30 to 35 minutes or
until an inserted toothpick comes out clean. Ice while
warm.

Icing

1 stick butter
4 tablespoons dark cocoa
6 tablespoons sour milk or buttermilk
1 teaspoon vanilla
1 box confectioner's sugar
3/4 cup nuts (optional)

Melt the butter and mix in the cocoa. Add the milk,
vanilla and sugar and mix until smooth. Stir in nuts.
Spread on top of cake.

Blackberry Jam Cake

1 cup sugar
3/4 cup shortening
3 eggs
1 cup blackberry jam, juice and all
1 teaspoon vanilla
1 teaspoon soda
1/2 cup buttermilk
1 teaspoon cloves
1 1/2 teaspoon cinnamon
1 teaspoon nutmeg
1 teaspoon baking powder
2 1/2 cups flour

Preheat oven to 375 degrees F. Sift dry ingredients together. Cream shortening and sugar. Add eggs one at a time, beating well. Add jam and vanilla. Add soda to buttermilk. Add buttermilk and dry ingredients, alternately to first mixture. Bake in three greased and floured 8 or 9 inch pans for 25 to 30 minutes.

Caramel Filling

3 cups sugar (2 cups white, 1 cup brown sugar)
2 tablespoons butter
1/2 teaspoon cinnamon
3/4 cup milk

Mix ingredients in saucepan; heat to soft ball stage. Briskly mix until creamy, but not hard. Spread thin layer between layers and on top. Do not overcook.

> ➤ *Mrs. Lee Macom, Dubach, shared this recipe. Icing adapted from a recipe from Mildred Swift, popular television host in Monroe in the 1960s.*

Fruit and Cheese Pastry

1 stick of butter
1/4 cup sugar
2 tablespoons milk
1 1/4 cups flour
4 ounces Swiss cheese (about 5 slices)
1 cup flaked coconut (optional)
About 3 cups sliced fresh seasonal fruit
1/2 to 1 cup jelly, preserves, or marmalade
1 tablespoon brandy or bourbon (optional)

Preheat oven to 350 degrees F. Put butter, sugar, milk,
flour and cheese in a processor and spin until mixture is
processed. It will look like a short dough that makes a
ball. Spread the dough by hand into a 12-inch pizza pan,
leaving a lip around the edge. If using coconut, sprinkle
on the crust. Bake for 15 to 20 minutes or until the crust
is lightly browned. While the crust is baking, slice the
fruit or combination of fruit. Arrange the fruit on the
warm crust. Dissolve the jelly and brandy in a saucepan.
Spread over the fruit. 10 servings.

> ➤ *Try making individual servings by using an ovenproof*
> *saucer or pan as a guide for shaping the dough.*

Lemon Pound Cake

3 cups all-purpose flour
3 cups granulated sugar
3 sticks butter, room temperature
8 eggs
1/2 cup lemon juice

Preheat oven to 325 degrees F. Combine flour and sugar in a large mixing bowl, and stir until well mixed. Add eggs, butter and lemon juice and mix well. Pour into a well-greased tube pan, and bake for 1 hour or until a toothpick inserted into the cake comes out clean. Invert the cake onto a plate. While the cake is still warm, prick the top with a toothpick in several places, and slowly pour the glaze over the cake. Cool before slicing.

Glaze

1/3 cup lemon juice
1/4 cup sugar

Heat the sugar and lemon juice in a small sauce pan. Stir constantly until the sugar dissolves. For a sweeter glaze, increase the amount of sugar.

According the LSU AgCenter, Meyers lemons are often grown successfully in Louisiana, because they are more cold-hearty than most varieties. They are a cross between an orange and a lemon. They are usually ready to be harvested in November and December.

Sweet Potato Bundt Cake
Kellie Trimble, Mr. Lester's
Cypress Bayou Casino, Charenton

2 medium peeled sweet potatoes
1.25 pound box of yellow cake mix
1 1/3 cups water
1/3 cup oil
4 whole eggs
2 tablespoons cinnamon
1 tablespoon nutmeg
1 tablespoon vanilla extract

Boil the sweet potatoes until fork tender and allow to cool. Mash the sweet potatoes before adding to the cake mix. Preheat oven to 350 degrees F. Prepare the cake mix (cake mix, oil, water, eggs). Then add the sweet potatoes and remaining spices. Add the brown sugar schmear to the bottom of a well-greased bundt or tube cake pan before adding the cake mix to the pan. Pour the mix on top of the schmear and bake for 40 to 50 minutes or until a toothpick comes out clean. Cool the cake before removing from the pan. Serves 10 to 12.

Schmear

1 stick butter, soft
2 cups light brown sugar
1 cup chopped pecans

Mix together all ingredients until smooth and add to the bottom of the Bundt cake pan before adding the batter.

Gateau Sirop
(Syrup Cake)

1 1/2 cups brown sugar
1 cup cane syrup
1 cup vegetable oil
1 cup boiling water
2 teaspoons baking soda
1 teaspoon vinegar
1 teaspoon cinnamon
1 teaspoon vanilla
2 1/2 cups flour
2 eggs, beaten well
1 cup toasted pecans

Preheat oven to 350 degrees F. Mix brown sugar, syrup and oil. In another bowl, mix boiling water, baking soda and vinegar. Add to the first bowl. Add cinnamon and vanilla. Gradually mix in portions of flour. Add eggs. Then stir in pecans. Bake about 40 minutes.

> ➤ *Ann Palombo shared this recipe. Gateau Sirop is a Cajun classic that uses cane syrup. The cake, similar to a spice cake, gets its unique texture from the syrup.*

Louisiana produces about 20 per cent of the sugar grown in the United States. Sugar cane, a type of grass, is planted using whole stalks, rather than seeds.

Carrot Cake

2 cups flour
2 teaspoons baking powder
2 teaspoons soda
2 teaspoons cinnamon
1 teaspoon salt
1 1/2 cups oil
3 cups grated raw carrots
2 cups sugar
4 eggs

Preheat oven to 300 degrees F. Combine flour, baking powder, soda, cinnamon, salt and sugar in a large mixing bowl. Stir in oil. Add grated carrots. Add eggs, one at a time, stirring well after each one. Spread into greased 13 x 9 inch baking pan. Bake for 45 minutes or until it tests done. Cool before frosting.

Icing

1 (8-ounce) package cream cheese
2 teaspoons vanilla
1/2 stick butter, softened
1 pound powdered sugar
1/2 cup chopped nuts, optional

Mix ingredients well and spread on cooled cake.

Pearl's Nut Cake

2 cups sugar
2 eggs
2 cups plain flour (1 cup may be whole wheat)
2 teaspoons soda
1 teaspoon salt
1 (20-ounce) can crushed pineapple, undrained
1 teaspoon vanilla
1/2 cup pecan pieces

Preheat oven to 350 degrees F. Spray 9 x 13 inch pan with Pam. Put all ingredients in a large mixing bowl and stir with a spoon until well mixed. Bake in oven for 35 to 40 minutes or until middle springs back when touched.

Icing

1 (8-ounce) package cream cheese
1/2 cup pecan pieces
1 3/4 cup powdered sugar
1 teaspoon vanilla
1 stick butter, melted

Mix ingredients well and spread on the warm cake. Cool before serving.

➤ *This delicious cake is deceptively easy to make.*

Chewy Plantation Pie
Classic Golden Pecans; www.classicgoldenpecans.com

3 whole eggs
1 cup dark brown sugar
1 cup light Karo corn syrup
1 1/2 cup chopped Classic Golden Chef's
      Choice Pecans (large pieces)
1 teaspoon vanilla extract
1 unbaked 9-inch pie shell
2 tablespoons bourbon whiskey*

Preheat oven to 225 degrees F. Beat eggs, add sugar,
syrup and Classic Golden Chef's Choice Pecans. Whip
in vanilla and bourbon and pour into unbaked pie shell.
Bake 90 minutes at 225 degrees F and 30 minutes at 300
degrees F. Cool before serving.

*This ingredient is not required. It is only a flavoring. When
added, all alcohol will fully evaporate in the baking process
leaving only the flavor.

The French created the pecan pie after settling in New
Orleans and being introduced to the pecan by Native
Americans. Today pecans are used in many desserts,
salads, breads, vegetables and entrée recipes.

Myrtis's Blonde Pecan Pie

1/2 cup butter, softened
1 cup granulated sugar, divided
3 tablespoons flour
2 eggs
1 cup all-purpose flour
2 tablespoons cream, half and half, or milk
1/2 teaspoon vanilla
1 cup chopped pecans

Preheat oven to 400 degrees F. Cream butter and 1/2 cup granulated sugar in a mixing bowl. Blend in 1 cup of flour well. Dough will be very dry. Press dough into a greased 9-inch pie pan. Set dough aside while making filling. Beat 2 eggs well by hand and mix in the other 1/2 cup granulated sugar, flour, cream and vanilla. Mix well. Add chopped pecans; stir. Pour the filling into the uncooked pie crust; bake 18 to 20 minutes or until crust edge browns lightly. Cool about 5 minutes. Serve with whipped cream or ice cream.

➤ *Myrtis McCutchan D'Aquin of Crowley created this recipe for a contest.*

Town Club Pie

1 1/2 sticks butter
3 squares unsweetened chocolate, chopped
3 eggs, beaten
2 cups confectioner's sugar
1 teaspoon vanilla
Dash salt
1 cup pecans, chopped
Graham cracker crust

Melt butter and add chocolate. When chocolate has melted, add eggs, stirring over low heat until well mixed. Add confectioner's sugar a little at a time, stirring constantly until the filling thickens. Remove from heat and add vanilla, salt and pecans. Pour into a graham cracker crust. Chill for several hours.

➤ *This recipe is based on a dessert served at the Crowley Town Club.*

Chess Pie

1 1/2 cups sugar
3 eggs, beaten lightly
1 teaspoon vinegar
1/2 teaspoon vanilla
1 tablespoon cornmeal
1 stick butter, melted

Preheat oven to 350 degrees F. Combine all ingredients in the order given. Stir enough to mix thoroughly. Do not beat. Pour in unbaked pie shell and bake 45 minutes.

Classic Pumpkin Pie

3/4 cup sugar
1/2 teaspoon salt
1 1/2 teaspoons ground cinnamon
1/2 teaspoon nutmeg
1/2 teaspoon ground cloves
1 (15-ounce) can pure pumpkin
2 eggs, beaten
1 1/2 cups half and half or evaporated milk
1 9-inch unbaked deep dish pie crust

Preheat oven to 425 degrees F. Combine sugar, salt and spices. Stir in pumpkin and eggs. Gradually add milk and stir until mixed well. Pour into pie shell. Bake at 425 degrees F for 15 minutes. Reduce temperature to 375 degrees F and bake for 40 to 50 minutes or until knife inserted in the center comes out clean. Delicious with whipped cream or ice cream.

Shortbread Cookies

1 cup soft butter
1/2 cup brown sugar
2 1/2 cups flour

Cream butter and sugar until light and fluffy. Stir in flour until well blended. Dough will be very stiff. Divide dough into two parts and shape into two rolls about two inches in diameter. Wrap in waxed paper and refrigerate several hours or overnight. To bake, slice into 1/4 inch slices and bake on ungreased cookie sheet in oven preheated to 300 degrees F for 25 minutes or until light golden. Makes about 4 dozen cookies.

Christmas Cream Cheese Cupcakes

3 (8-ounce) packages cream cheese, room
temperature
1 1/2 cups sugar, separated
5 eggs
1/2 teaspoon vanilla
1/4 cup sour cream
Jar maraschino cherries
2 dozen cupcake liners

Preheat oven to 325 degrees F and place cupcake liners
in two muffin pans. Mix the cream cheese, 1 cup of
sugar, eggs and vanilla with electric mixer until smooth.
Fill cupcake liners three-fourths full. Bake in oven for 45
minutes. While baking, mix the sour cream and 1/2 cup
of sugar with a spoon until well combined. Remove from
oven. Cupcakes will sink in the middle. Put one
teaspoon filling and one whole maraschino cherry on
top of each cupcake. Return to oven for additional 5
minutes. Cool and refrigerate. Makes two dozen.

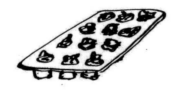

White Chocolate Brownies
Patti Constantin, Designs in Catering, New Orleans

14 tablespoons unsalted butter
16 ounces white chocolate, finely chopped
    or shredded
4 eggs, room temperature
Pinch of salt
1 cup sugar
3 teaspoons vanilla
2 cups flour
8 ounces (2 cups) bittersweet chocolate chunks

Preheat oven to 350 degrees F. Line the bottom and two sides of 8 inch pan with aluminum foil (For thinner brownies, use 9 x 13 inch pan). Lightly grease foil. In saucepan, melt butter. Remove from heat. Add half of the white chocolate. Do not stir; let mixture sit. In large mixing bowl, combine eggs and salt. Beat until frothy. Gradually add sugar and beat for 2 minutes. Add white chocolate and butter mixture, vanilla and flour. Quickly beat until smooth. Stir in remaining white chocolate and bittersweet chocolate chunks. Put batter in pan and bake 35 to 40 minutes. Cool for 4 hours before cutting.

> ➢ *New Orleans chef and caterer Patti Constantin serves this decadent brownie recipe at catered events. This recipe was served in her restaurant, Constantins, where it was a popular dessert choice for diners.*

Brownies

3 (1-ounce) unsweetened baking squares
1/2 cup butter
1 1/2 cups sugar
3 eggs
1 cup flour
Pinch of salt
1/2 teaspoon baking powder
1 teaspoon vanilla
1 cup semisweet chocolate chips
1/2 cup pecans or walnuts, chopped (optional)

Preheat oven to 350 degrees F. Line 8-inch baking pan with lightly greased aluminum foil, edges sticking up, or grease with butter and lightly dust with flour. Melt chocolate and butter in double boiler, stirring as mixture melts. Put sugar in medium size mixing bowl. When chocolate and butter are melted, add to sugar and blend well. Add eggs one at a time and stir into mixture. Mix dry ingredients together and stir into chocolate mix. Stir in vanilla, nuts and chocolate chips. Pour mixture into pan and bake in preheated oven for 35 to 40 minutes. Brownies are done when wooden pick inserted in center comes out clean. Cool on rack completely before cutting. Grab sides of aluminum foil and lift out of pan.

> ➤ *For a richer tasting brownie, substitute 1 and 1/2 teaspoons Steen's Syrup for the vanilla.*

> ➤ *To prevent crumbling, use a plastic knife when cutting brownies.*

Fresh Lemon Squares

Crust

2 cups flour
1/2 cup confectioner's sugar
1/2 pound cold butter

Preheat oven to 350 degrees F. Combine all ingredients in a food processor until crumbly. Press into a 9 x 13 inch pan. Bake for 20 minutes. Remove from oven and allow to cool five to ten minutes.

Filling

4 eggs, lightly beaten
1/4 cup flour
2 cups granulated sugar
1/2 teaspoon baking powder
Zest of squeezed lemons
1/2 cup lemon juice (zest lemon first, then
       squeeze)

In medium mixing bowl, beat all ingredients together. Pour over baked crust. Bake for 25 minutes. When completely cool, cut into squares and sprinkle top with confectioner's sugar.

> ➤ *Former Louisiana resident Kathy Phelps adapted her mother's recipe to use fresh lemons rather than bottled or frozen lemon juice.*

Aunt Tina's Praline Cookies

1 2/3 cups all-purpose flour
1 1/2 teaspoons baking powder
1/2 teaspoon salt
1 stick unsalted butter
1 1/2 cups light brown sugar, firmly packed
1 large egg
1 teaspoon pure vanilla extract

Preheat oven to 350 degrees F. Sift together flour, baking powder and salt in a medium bowl. Set aside. In bowl of electric mixer fitted with the paddle attachment, cream butter and brown sugar on medium speed until light and fluffy, about 2 minutes. Add egg and vanilla. Beat until fully combined. Add dry ingredients and beat on low speed until combined. Drop batter by rounded teaspoons onto ungreased baking sheet about two inches apart. Bake until firm and barely golden, 10 to 12 minutes. Transfer pan to cool for five minutes and then transfer cookies to wire rack. Top with praline topping when cool.

Praline Topping

3/4 cup light brown sugar
3/4 cup white sugar
1/2 cup evaporated milk
2 tablespoons butter
1 teaspoon vanilla
1/2 cup chopped pecans

Mix both sugars with evaporated milk in boiler and bring to a boil. Cook on medium-high about 6 minutes, stirring frequently. Turn off heat and mix in 2

(continued)
tablespoons butter and vanilla. Mix until well blended.
Add pecans and drop mixture onto tops of cookies.
Mixture will harden when it cools. Store in airtight
container.

> ➤ *Recipe from Cindy Clark, Lafayette.*

Tea Cakes

1/2 cup butter
1 cup sugar
1 tablespoon milk
2 eggs, beaten
2 teaspoons baking powder
2 1/4 cups flour
1/4 teaspoon salt
1 teaspoon vanilla

Preheat oven to 400 degrees F. Cream butter and sugar.
Add beaten eggs, vanilla, milk and dry ingredients.
Dough will be very stiff. Dough can be refrigerated to
help make rolling out easier. Roll out dough to about
1/4 inch thick. Cut into circles and place on greased
baking sheet. Sprinkle tops with granulated sugar. Bake
for 10 minutes. For crispier cookies, reduce heat to 350
degrees F, and bake for 12 to 15 minutes. Cookies are
done when edges are just beginning to turn brown. Tops
will be light color.

> ➤ *These cookies are a Southern favorite. Some like them*
> *crispy; some like them soft. Whether you cut them thin*
> *or thick, large or small, these cookies are delicious with*
> *coffee or tea. Recipe from Fran Roberson, Dubach.*

Oma's Lebkuchen Cookies

1 cup honey
1/3 cup blanched, chopped almonds
3/4 cup brown sugar
2 1/2 cups flour, sifted
1 egg, well beaten
1/2 teaspoon soda
1 tablespoon lemon juice
1/2 teaspoon allspice
1 tablespoon grated lemon rind
1/2 teaspoon cinnamon
1/3 cup chopped citron
1/2 teaspoon cloves

Bring honey to a boil in small pan; pour into a mixing bowl to cool. Add remaining ingredients. Mix well. Wrap dough in plastic wrap and store overnight in the refrigerator. When ready to bake, preheat oven to 400 degrees F. Place dough on floured board (dough is sticky, so keep unused portion in refrigerator). Roll out to 1/2 inch thick. Use cookie cutters to cut out cookies about 2 inches across, or smaller. Place on greased cookie sheet about 2 inches apart. Bake for 10 to 12 minutes. When cool, ice with thin icing and decorate with thinly sliced almonds and citron. Dough can also be baked in a pan like gingerbread.

Germans settled upriver from New Orleans in the early 1700s in an area called the German Coast. Roberts Cove is another town originally settled by Germans. Christmas traditionally arrived December 5 in Roberts Cove with a visit from St. Nicholas. The St. Nicholas celebration was discontinued during WWII, but has been revived in recent years.

Christmas Eve Rum Balls
Kent and Libby Follette, Follette Pottery
Pea Ridge Road, Dubach

1 (5 1/4-ounce) package tootsie roll candy
1/3 cup rum (dark Haitian rum is wonderful)
2 tablespoons butter
1 2/3 cups graham cracker crumbs
1 cup crushed pecans
1 cup powdered sugar

Combine candy, rum and butter in saucepan. Heat and stir until melted and smooth. Stir in crumbs and nuts. Shape to form 1 inch balls (mixture will be hot). Roll in powdered sugar. Let cool and store in airtight container.

➤ *For almost 40 years, this recipe has been a part of Christmas tradition in the Follette home. Libby makes the Rum Balls every Christmas Eve.*

Grandma McCutchan's Penuche Nuts

1 cup brown sugar
1/2 cup granulated sugar
1/2 cup sour cream
1 teaspoon vanilla
2 1/2 cups pecans

Combine both sugars and sour cream in a pot. On low to medium heat, stir constantly until the sugars dissolve. Cook until mixture is at soft-ball stage or registers 236 degrees on a candy thermometer. Remove from heat. Add pecans and vanilla. Stir until sugar forms a coating on the nuts. Take out and place individual nuts or a small clump of nuts on pieces of waxed paper. Cool.

> ➢ *This candy, also spelled "penuchi, panocha, panoche," serves as a vivid reminder of my white-haired Grandma McCutchan driving on I-10 from Lake Charles to Lafayette, across a small swamp to spend Christmas with us, loaded with her batches of various treats. Her arrival signaled that Christmas had arrived. –Ann Palombo*

The annual Louisiana Sugar Cane Festival is held each September in New Iberia. Sugar cane farmers are honored with a boat parade, fireworks and two parades down historic Main Street. On Sunday, Mass is held to bless the crops as farmers begin harvest season.

Marshmallow and Pecan Stuffed Dates
Sarah Liberta, HERBS by Sarah, Baton Rouge
www.herbsbysarah.com

24 dates, preferably Medjool
12 marshmallows, cut in half
24 large pecan halves
Powdered sugar

If the dates contain pits, use a paring knife to make a slit in each date sufficient to remove the pit. Place one marshmallow half in each date, cut side up. Top with a pecan half. Arrange on a platter or cheese tray. Dust with powdered sugar just before serving. Dates may be made ahead and stored in sealed plastic cartons or tins. Don't use powdered sugar until ready to serve, or the sugar will be absorbed. Makes 12 to 24 servings

> ➢ *These dates were a favorite at all our holiday parties when I was growing up. I think they derive from a traditional Italian treat often served in my father's family.—Sarah Liberta*

Bourbon Praline Sauce for Ice Cream

1/4 cup butter
1 cup packed brown sugar
1 cup pecan pieces
1 tablespoon light corn syrup
1/4 cup bourbon

Melt butter in a heavy skillet. Add sugar, pecans and syrup. Bring to a boil, stirring constantly. Reduce heat and cook for 1 minute. Stir in bourbon. Store in a covered jar in the refrigerator.

Date Nut Roll

1 cup sugar
1 cup brown sugar
1 cup milk
1/2 pound dates, chopped
1 cup pecans or walnuts, chopped

Heat sugars and milk in small saucepan until soft-ball stage (235 to 240 degrees F). Place chopped dates in bowl and pour milk mixture over dates. Let cool. Stir mixture until it begins to harden. Add nuts. Mix well. Form mixture into a roll and wrap in waxed paper. Store in refrigerator until hardened. Slice thinly to serve.

Peanut Brittle

2 cups sugar
1 cup light Karo syrup
1/2 cup water
1 pound small peanuts
1 teaspoon butter
1 teaspoon soda

Lightly grease cookie sheet. Heat sugar, corn syrup and water in saucepan. Bring to a boil and bring to 236 degrees F on a candy thermometer. Add peanuts and continue to heat until mixture reaches 290 degrees F and peanuts begin to crack. Remove from heat. Add butter and soda and stir quickly. Pour mixture onto prepared cookie sheet while still foamy. Allow to cool and then break into pieces. Store in air tight container.

> ➤ *These recipes are courtesy of Pam Stroup of Lafayette. Recipes are originally from her aunt Mildred Jones.*

Easy Microwave Pralines

1 cup whipping cream
1 pound light brown sugar
2 cups pecan halves
2 tablespoons butter, cut up and room
    temperature

Mix cream and brown sugar in large microwave safe bowl (about 4-quart size). Microwave on high 11 to 13 minutes (227 degrees, soft-ball stage). Remove from microwave and stir in pecans and butter. Drop by teaspoons onto sheets of foil to cool.

Simply Delicious Praline Cookies

30 graham cracker squares
1 cup brown sugar, packed
2 sticks butter
2 cups pecans, chopped
1 teaspoon vanilla

Preheat oven to 350 degrees F. Cover ungreased cookie sheet with single layer of graham crackers. Combine sugar and butter in a saucepan; heat until butter melts, stirring constantly. Continue heating and stirring for 1 minute. Remove from heat. Add pecans and vanilla. Spread mixture evenly over the graham crackers. Bake for 10 minutes or until bubbling. Slice while warm.

Pralines originated in France where they were made with sugar and almonds, but in Louisiana, they are usually made with pecans. The candy has been popular since the mid-1700s and can be found in convenience stores, as well as in fine bakeries.

Chocolate Fudge

2 cups sugar
2/3 cup evaporated skimmed milk
12 regular marshmallows
1/2 cup butter
Dash of salt
1 (6-ounce) package semi-sweet chocolate pieces
1 teaspoon vanilla
1 cup chopped pecans or walnuts

Mix sugar, milk, marshmallows, salt and butter in a
heavy 2-quart saucepan. Cook, stirring constantly over
medium heat until mixture boils. Boil and stir for 5
minutes. Remove from heat and stir in chocolate chips
until completely melted. Stir in nuts and vanilla. Pour
into a buttered 8-inch pan. Cool.

Cotton Country Divinity

3 cups sugar
1 cup water
1/2 cup white Karo syrup
2 egg whites, room temperature
1 tablespoon vanilla

Mix sugar, water and syrup in medium saucepan. Stir
until blended. Do not stir as you bring to a boil and
cook to 238 degrees F. Beat egg whites in medium bowl
until soft peaks form. Gradually add 1/2 cup of syrup
mixture. Cook remainder of syrup mixture to 258
degrees F. Add to egg mixture. Add vanilla and beat
mixture until it begins to lose its gloss. Drop by teaspoon
on waxed paper. Optional: top each piece with a pecan
half.

Hanley-Gueno Neapolitan Presepio; Lafayette, Louisiana

Les Menus Spéciaux

Game Day Menu

Snacks
Rosemary Walnuts (p. 44)
Southern Ambrosia (p. 63)
Veggies with Rosemary Cheese Dip (p. 43)
Hearty Queso Dip with Tortilla Chips (p. 38)
Southern Sausage Balls (p. 37)

Main Course
Game Day Pistolettes (p. 124)
Spicy Louisiana Cole Slaw (p. 66)
Bill's Spicy Baked Beans (p. 87)

Dessert
Brownies (p. 150)
Fresh Lemon Squares (p. 151)

Game Day in Louisiana comes in many colors: purple and gold, red and white, blue and red, black and gold, blue and gold and more. Whatever the colors, the day is filled with anticipation and excitement. Whether you are watching the game at home or tailgating in the stadium, menus should include quick and easy, make-ahead foods that guests can serve themselves. Use paper products for easy clean up, and enjoy the game!

Brunch Menu

Sweet Dishes
Spiced Fruit Compote (p. 173)
Praline Pecan Crunch (p. 175)

Savory Dishes
Christmas Morning Sausage Rolls (p. 56)
Make-Ahead Breakfast Casserole (p. 59)
Bagels and Smoked Salmon Spread (p. 43)

Baked Goods
Pumpkin Bread (p. 47)
Apple Cranberry Muffins (p.46)

Beverages
Juice
Café au Lait
Hot Chocolate with peppermint sticks

The Christmas breakfast or brunch menu should reflect the warmth of the season. Plan a menu to include the aroma of fresh coffee or food baking in the oven. Give yourself a break. Make things ahead and take time to enjoy the morning.

Réveillon Menu

First Course
Shrimp Cocktail: Boiled Shrimp (p. 41) with
      Nina's New Orleans Remoulade Sauce (p. 41)

Second Course
Olive Citrus Salad (p. 64)
Crispy French Bread (p. 54)

Third Course
Instant or Fresh Cranberry Relish (p. 62)
Seafood Stuffed Turkey Breast (p. 106)
      with Tomato Cream Sauce (p. 107)
Sweet Potato Casserole (p. 91)
Green Beans with Almonds (p. 87)
Bonanno's Italian Sausage Rice Dressing (p. 98)
No Knead Wheat Rolls (p. 60)

Fourth Course
Chewy Plantation Pie (p. 144)
Town Club Pie (p. 146)
Whipped Cream Topping (optional)

Christmas is a time for enjoying special meals with family and friends. Whether you have a big meal for Christmas Eve after midnight Mass in the Réveillon tradition or on Christmas Day, the menu may include everything from traditional favorites to something new. Make things festive and plan ahead, so everyone can sit down and enjoy the meal.

Hanley-Gueno Neapolitan Presepio; Lafayette, Louisiana

Lagniappe

Mulled Cider
Sarah Liberta, HERBS by Sarah, Baton Rouge
www.herbsbysarah.com

1/2 gallon apple cider
1 tablespoon HERBS by Sarah Mulling Spices (whole
   cinnamon, cloves, allspice, coriander seed,
   star anise)

Pour cider into a large stainless steel or enamel pot. Place spices in a small muslin bag or a stainless steel tea strainer and add to pot. Bring to a boil, lower fire, and simmer for 1 hour. Allow to cool slightly before serving. Pour into a punch bowl and garnish with slices of orange studded with cloves. Or serve in mugs with cinnamon stick stirrers. Also delicious chilled. Makes 8 to 10 servings.

➤ *This wonderfully warm beverage fills the house with great aromas to greet your guests—Sarah Liberta*

Sangria

1 gallon Burgundy
48 ounces apple juice
5 cups orange juice
2 cups sugar
1 cups Rose's Lime Juice

Mix all ingredients together and refrigerate until ready to serve. Serve with fresh orange slices as garnish.

Mimosa, Azalea and Camellia

1 bottle champagne, sparkling wine
    or sparkling water
1 quart cranberry juice
1 quart orange juice

Mix about 3 parts champagne or sparkling water or wine
with orange juice to make a Mimosa. To make an Azalea,
use cranberry juice; to make a Camellia mix equal parts
cranberry and orange juice with the champagne.
Measurements are not exact, so if you prefer less alcohol, use
more juice. If you have fresh mint, add a sprig to each glass.

Citrus Eye Opener

1 (12-ounce) can frozen orange juice concentrate
1 (6-ounce) can frozen lemonade concentrate
1 (2-liter) bottle carbonated water
1 orange, cut into wedges
1 cup water

In a one-gallon container combine both concentrates and
the cup of water. Cover container and chill until serving
time. Just before serving, slowly add carbonated water. Stir
gently. Serve over ice. Hook orange wedges on the side of
each glass or, if serving as a punch, float the slices in the
punch. Makes 8 to 10 servings.

Almost every Louisiana celebration includes music. The
diverse styles include African-American song, rural blues,
Cajun fiddling at the fais-do-dos, the Creole Zydeco
tradition, the community hymn singing of North Louisiana,
urban jazz and the Dixieland music played by bands at
Preservation Hall in New Orleans.

Ralph's Egg Nog

6 eggs*
1 cup extra-fine baking sugar
1/2 teaspoon vanilla extract
1/2 teaspoon grated nutmeg
2 1/2 cups heavy whipping cream
2 cups whole milk
1/2 cup brandy
1/2 cup dark rum

Beat eggs until frothy, adding sugar and continuing to beat. Add nutmeg and vanilla and continue beating. Slowly add in whipping cream and then milk, continuing to beat well while adding. Beat in alcohol, and then chill well. Serve with a dollop of whipped cream on top with a sprinkle of grated nutmeg.

*NOTE: Use caution when using raw eggs. Always use fresh eggs with shells intact. For extra caution, heat eggs with cream, milk and sugar to 160 degrees F, cool mixture and then continue with recipe.

> ➤ *My dad always served this on Christmas Eve from an antique milk glass footed bowl. He was raised in New Orleans, but lived most of his adult life in Lake Charles. He always beat the ingredients by hand, but when I have made it I use an electric mixer. It is very rich and quite delicious.—Peggy Reeves, Lafayette*

Champoreau

1 cup of brewed coffee
1/4 to 1/2 cup of milk, heated
Rum, bourbon or other alcohol

Make café au lait with coffee and milk. Add rum or other alcohol to taste.

> ➢ *This simple drink was popular with early French settlers in Louisiana.*

Milk Punch

2 cups whole milk
1/2 cup half and half
1/2 cup powdered sugar
1 cup bourbon or brandy
1 teaspoon vanilla extract
Freshly grated nutmeg

Mix first five ingredients together until sugar is well blended. To make the drink slushy, put in freezer for a couple of hours before serving. Otherwise, chill in refrigerator. Serve with grated nutmeg on top.

Milk punch dates back to Benjamin Franklin and has long been a popular holiday drink in New Orleans. Be careful when serving and warn guests that the drinks may taste like a milk shake, but they are potent.

Coffee Punch

1/2 (2-ounce) jar instant coffee, or more
1 cup sugar
2 cups hot water
4 quarts milk
2 quarts vanilla ice cream
2 quarts of chocolate ice cream

Blend coffee, sugar and hot water. Let cool. Add milk and softened vanilla and chocolate ice cream. Fill punch bowl.

> ➤ *This punch is rich and thick and delicious.*

Christmas Punch

8 cups chilled cranberry juice cocktail
2 cups brandy
1 (6-ounce) can frozen orange juice
1 (6-ounce) can frozen pineapple juice
2 fifths chilled white champagne
Ice mold (with frozen fruit optional)

All ingredients except champagne and ice mold can be assembled in advance. Add champagne and ice mold at beginning of party. Makes 30 servings.

Cappuccino Mix

3 1/2 cups dry milk
1/2 cup cocoa
2 1/2 cups sugar
1 teaspoon cinnamon
1 1/2 cup instant coffee

Mix all ingredients. Use 1 tablespoon for each 6-ounce cup of hot water.

> ➤ *Hot chocolate mixes are popular during the holidays. Make this mix to have on hand for guests or to give to teachers and friends as a gift from your kitchen.*

Mocha Hot Chocolate

2 squares unsweetened chocolate
1 cup strong coffee
3 tablespoons sugar
Dash of salt
3 cups milk
Whipped cream (optional)

Melt chocolate in 1 cup of coffee over very low heat. Stir constantly while adding sugar and salt. Continue stirring until it boils. Lower heat; simmer 3 minutes. Gradually add milk; heat thoroughly. Just before serving, beat with rotary beater. Serve with whipped cream, if desired.

Hot Spiced Tea

1 cup sugar
7 cups water
1 stick cinnamon
1/2 cup orange juice
1/2 cup pineapple juice
1/4 cup lemon juice
6 tea bags

Combine 1 cup water with sugar and cinnamon; boil 5 minutes. Steep tea bags in 6 cups hot water 5 minutes. Remove bags. Combine juices, hot sugar syrup and hot tea. Grated rind may be added, if desired. For a mild cinnamon flavor, remove stick from syrup before adding juices and tea. Serve piping hot. Makes 10 to 12 servings.

Satsuma Honey Butter

1/2 cup butter, softened
1/4 cup honey
2 teaspoons of satsuma zest

Cream butter until light and fluffy. Slowly add honey and beat well. Beat in satsuma zest. Serve with biscuits, toast, waffles or pancakes.

> ➤ *Substitute orange zest if satsumas are not available.*

Spiced Fruit Compote
Sarah Liberta, HERBS by Sarah; www.herbsbysarah.com

3 apples, peeled and cut into slices or 1-inch cubes
3 pears, peeled and cut into slices or 1-inch cubes
3 peaches, peeled and cut into slices or 1-inch cubes
1/2 cup apple juice or cider (optional)
1 cup brown sugar
1 teaspoon cinnamon, freshly ground if possible
1/4 teaspoon nutmeg, freshly ground if possible
1/4 teaspoon allspice, freshly ground if possible
1/2 stick butter or margarine

Combine all ingredients in a large, heavy-bottomed pot and cook over medium heat until the mixture comes to a boil. Reduce heat and simmer for about half an hour, or until fruit reaches desired consistency. Serve warm or at room temperature. Makes 6 to 8 servings.

➤ *One of my mother's favorite holiday meals was sandwiches of smoked turkey and Swiss cheese with horseradish mayonnaise on warm yeasty finger rolls, served with spiced peaches. I love it, too, and it inspired me to experiment with other spiced fruits. This is more a technique than a recipe. Use whatever fruits you prefer or have on hand, fresh or canned. While the compote is a great side to accompany holiday poultry, it can easily become a dessert or the basis for a trifle. Add a topper, and you have an upside-down cake, a fruit crisp, or a cobbler. Experiment and enjoy!—Sarah Liberta*

Chocolate Fudge Sauce

2 squares unsweetened chocolate
1/8 teaspoon cream of tartar
Dash of salt
1 1/2 cups sugar
1 cup evaporated milk
1 teaspoon vanilla

Melt chocolate in small pan over low heat or in double boiler. Add cream of tartar and salt. Stir in milk and sugar alternately. Continue stirring and heating over medium heat until smooth. Stir in vanilla. Store in the refrigerator, and use as a sauce on hot or cold desserts.

> ➤ *Keep this on hand during the holidays. Add nuts, and drizzle over ice cream for a quick and delicious dessert.*

Quick Energy Treat

1 cup oatmeal
1/2 cup dark chocolate chips
1/2 cup natural peanut butter
1/2 cup flaxseeds
1/3 cup honey
1/3 cup dried cranberries
1/2 cup chopped pecans or other nuts
1 teaspoon vanilla

Mix all ingredients together. Chill at least 30 minutes. Roll into balls. Store in refrigerator. Makes about 24.

> ➤ *Lafayette Pilates instructor Susan Thevenet contributed this holiday pick-me-up.*

Praline Pecan Crunch

1 box Quaker Squares (toasted oatmeal cereal)
2 cups coarsely chopped pecans
1/2 cup corn syrup
1/2 cup brown sugar
1/2 stick butter
1 teaspoon vanilla
1/2 teaspoon baking soda

Preheat oven to 250 degrees F. Lightly grease 9 x 13 inch pan. Combine cereal and pecans in pan. Mix sugar, corn syrup and butter in microwave safe bowl. Microwave for 1 1/2 minutes, stir and then microwave another 30 seconds (should be boiling). Stir in vanilla and soda. Pour mixture over cereal and stir to coat evenly. Bake 1 hour, stirring every 20 minutes. Bake another 20 minutes. Spread on baking sheet to cool. Break into pieces and store in airtight container. Makes 9 cups.

➢ *Nancy Chustz of New Roads makes Praline Pecan Crunch every Christmas, dividing the mix into small bags or containers to give to friends and family.*

Guy's Mustard
Patti Constantin, Designs in Catering, New Orleans

1 cup brown vinegar
1/2 cup brown sugar
1/2 cup white sugar
1 cup dry mustard
3 eggs
Dijon mustard

Mix sugars and vinegar in bowl until dissolved. Fold in dry mustard a little at a time until blended. Add eggs and whip. Cook in double boiler and stir until heated thoroughly. Add equal part of Dijon mustard to the mustard mixture. Store in refrigerator.

Mushroom Sauce

1/4 cup onions
1/4 cup chopped mushrooms
1 tablespoon butter
1/4 cup chicken stock
1/2 cup white wine
1/4 cup cooked shrimp
1/4 cup plain yogurt

Sauté onions and mushrooms in butter over low heat until they wilt. Add chicken stock, white wine, cooked shrimp and yogurt to the mixture. Simmer about 10 to 15 minutes, stirring occasionally. Serve over fish, seafood, meat or vegetables.

Refrigerator Pickles

5 to 8 thinly sliced cucumbers (about 6 cups)
2 cups granulated sugar
2 cups cider vinegar
1 cup water
1 cup onion, sliced thinly
1 cup bell pepper, chopped
1 teaspoon celery seed
2 tablespoons sea salt or pickling salt
4 wide mouth pint jars

Wash and slice cucumbers. Combine sugar, water, salt and vinegar in medium pan and heat to dissolve. Add onion, bell pepper and celery seed. Place sliced cucumbers in wide-mouth jars. Pack tightly. Pour liquid with onion and bell pepper over cucumber to fill jars. Put on lids and place in the refrigerator. Chill 24 hours. Will keep for about 2 weeks.

> ➤ Note: Use firm narrow cucumbers for best results. Try adding cauliflower or carrots.

ESPRIT DE NOËL

Great-grandmothers tell of the excitement of decorating the tree on Christmas Eve and the thrill of finding an orange or a trinket in their stockings Christmas Day. Much of the joy of Christmas is in the anticipation of what's to come and the preparations for the day. Small gifts in a stocking and simple activities like making decorations or wrapping gifts together can become lasting memories. Expectations and customs may change, but the spirit of Christmas continues as each generation creates its own memories and traditions.

Hanley-Gueno Neapolitan Presepio; Lafayette, Louisiana

Fun from the Pantry

Many common kitchen items can be used to create fun activities for children.

Potpourri Orange:

Oranges
Whole cloves

Stick cloves into oranges, covering the surface. Place them in a bowl or tie a ribbon and hang to enjoy the fresh scent or put each in a plastic sandwich bag, tie with a ribbon and give to friends.

Making Butter:

Clean baby food jars with lids or small mason jars
Heavy whipping cream
Clean marbles
Salt

Fill each jar about 1/3 full with whipping cream. Add two or three marbles. Seal lid. Have children shake the jars until they make butter. If not using the butter immediately, rinse with cool water until water runs clear. Store in refrigerator. A pinch of salt may be added.

Coffee Filter Snowflakes:

Round coffee filters, flattened
Scissors

Fold flattened coffee filter in half and then in half again. Cut shapes out of sides with scissors. Unwrap and hang from ribbon or tape on windows to create a winter scene.

Advent Wreath

An Advent wreath is a wonderful way to involve children in celebrating Christmas. It helps mark the season of Advent, beginning the fourth Sunday before Christmas and ending on Christmas Day. As candles are lit each Sunday, many families enjoy time together with Christmas music, stories or devotions. Candle colors vary in different traditions, but are usually four purple candles and one white or three purple, one pink and one white.

> 5 candles: 1 white votive or pillar candle, 1 pink and 3 purple taper candles
> 1 candle holder or stand
> Glue
> 1 Styrofoam wreath (or a frame from a hobby store)
> Evergreens, fresh or artificial

Place the ring on a table. Make holes for four candles, spaced equally apart. Place colored candles securely in wreath with a dab of glue in the bottom of each hole. The white candle will go in the center in a holder. Place greenery around the wreath to cover the Styrofoam. Add decorations, if desired.

Lighting the Wreath

On the first Sunday of Advent, light one of the purple candles during dinner or family devotion. In some traditions, the first candle represents Hope. After dinner, extinguish the candle. On the next three Sundays, light an additional candle along with the others that have been lit. The candles may represent Love, Joy and Peace. On Christmas Day, light all the candles, including the white candle to signify the birth of Christ.

Crystal Stars
(picture shown on page 3)

Help children create a Christmas wonderland with these sparkly stars.

> String
> Deep glass container
> White pipe cleaners
> Borax, 3 tablespoons for each cup of water
> Small dowel or pencil
> Boiling water
> Scissors

Cut a pipe cleaner into three equal sections, and twist the sections together at their centers to form a six-sided star shape. Fill the deep container with boiling water, and add the borax one tablespoon at a time to the boiling water, stirring to dissolve after each addition. Use 3 tablespoons borax for each cup of water. Tie a piece of string to the shaped pipe cleaner. Tie the other end of the string to the small dowel. The dowel should be long enough to span the container. The length of the string should be long enough for the star shaped pipe cleaner to be completely submerged into the borax solution. The star should hang freely without touching the side of the container. Leave it several hours or overnight. By morning, crystals will be formed on the pipe cleaner. The star can be hung as a tree decoration or in a window to catch the sunlight.

> ➤ *The pipe cleaners can be made into various Christmas shapes. Borax is found in the laundry soap section of most grocery stores.*

NEAPOLITAN PRESEPIO

The wonder of Christmas is vividly symbolized in the Hanley-Gueno Neapolitan Presepio. The display shows street scenes typical of the bustling daily life in Eighteenth-Century Naples. Merchants sell wares; women go to the market; children ride a donkey; a man plays a musical instrument. Inside the houses, people prepare food and gather around a table. There are animals, children, old people and young people sharing and interacting in the everyday busyness of life. In the midst of this activity is the glorious Nativity—Mary, Joseph and baby Jesus, the Wise Men, shepherds, angels—holiness in the midst of life.

For us, this is Christmas— Immanuel, God with us.

INDEX

Yams